COLLEGE SMART®

COLLEGE SMART®

Be Ready, Graduate On Time, and Save Everyone Lots of Money!

ROBERT R. NEUMAN, PhD

ISBN: 978-1-5114-8048-2
ISBN: 978-0-9961385-0-5

Editing: Jude Neuman
Design & Layout: AuthorsSupport.com
Infographics: Molly Quirk

for Jude

*"Education is not the filling of a pail,
but the lighting of a fire."*

—William Butler Yeats

Table of Contents

GET THE FACTS!

Study Time Expected by Professors

25–30 hours / week
Only **7% students** study this much!

Study Time Among College-bound Seniors in High School

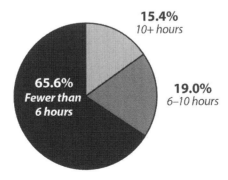

15.4%
10+ hours

19.0%
6–10 hours

65.6%
Fewer than 6 hours

Students not prepared for college study
Most study less than an hour a day
Learn what you should do

1 of 4 College Freshman Drop Out

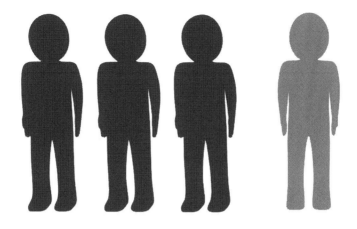

Top 10 Reasons Students
Leave/Drop Out of College

❶ Too much fun; not enough study.

❷ Homesick and feeling isolated.

❸ Academically unprepared.

❹ Financial constraints.

❺ Personal family issues.

❻ Academic climate.

❼ Lack of advice or guidance.

❽ Chose wrong area of study.

❾ Part-time job/work demands.

❿ Moved/new location.

This book covers all of these issues!

College Preparedness
When first-year students arrive on campus…

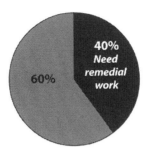

40%
Need remedial work

60%

According to college faculty, the number of incoming freshmen not ready to do college-level work.

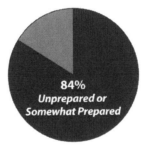

84%
Unprepared or Somewhat Prepared

Look at the grades students earned in high school.

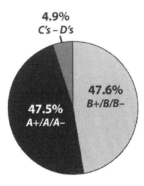

4.9%
C's – D's

47.6%
B+/B/B–

47.5%
A+/A/A–

What's wrong with this picture?
College is <u>NOT</u> high school away from home.

Education and Earnings Estimates for Full-Time Year-Round Workers

Millions of Dollars

Not high school graduate	High school graduate	Some college	Associate's degree	Bachelor's degree	Master's degree	Professional degree	Doctoral degree
$1.0	$1.2	$1.5	$1.6	$2.1	$2.5	$4.4	$3.4

The "layered" approach to learning

❶ Read ahead. That way…

❷ When the teacher presents the material, the class becomes a review for you.

❸ Then, ask good questions.

❹ Listen to the teacher and take good quality notes.

❺ Study after class and rework notes.

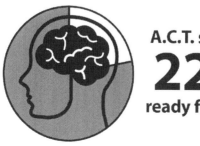

A.C.T. says only

22%
ready for college

Kids spend an average of 53+ hours a week with digital media.

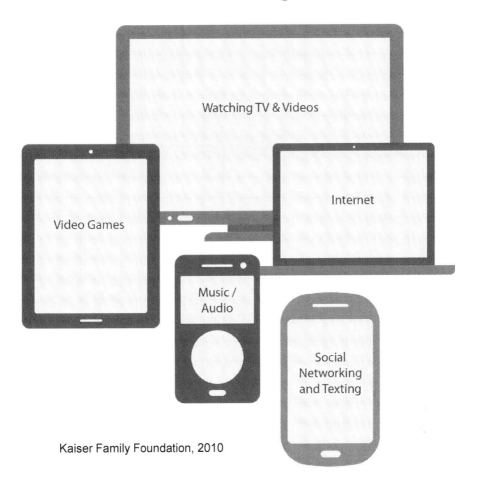

Watching TV & Videos

Video Games

Internet

Music / Audio

Social Networking and Texting

Kaiser Family Foundation, 2010

Dangerous Ideas Many High School Students Accept as True:

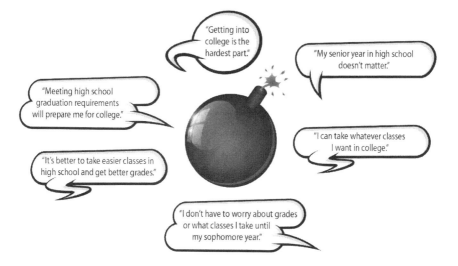

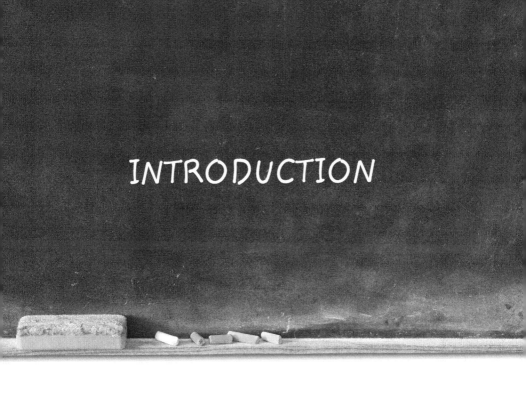

INTRODUCTION

Why you need this book

(You Really Do. Take My Word for It.)

· ·

Where are you in school? It makes no difference. This book is for you. All students do the same basic things, no matter their level of school. True, studying and learning get harder as you move from one year to the next. That's the way it's supposed to be. As you move on, you're expected to learn more and more each year. You're getting smarter, so you're able to do more. It just makes sense. Right?

Okay, let's keep going.

Let me ask you a question. How much do you like being a student: studying, learning, going to class, and so forth?

I'll give you three choices:

- A lot. It's great.
- It's okay. I can do it if I have to.
- If I could, I'd rather do something else.

So which did you choose?

If you chose #1, keep doing what you're doing. But if you chose #2 or #3, I want you to be like #1. This book will get you there. And you'll enjoy learning. In fact, science tells us you'll actually <u>crave</u> learning new things.

If you follow what I tell you in this book, you'll like being a student more and more.

- You'll like all of your courses.
- You'll get rid of lots of stress.
- You'll get higher grades.
- You'll always look forward to your next year.

Believe me: I'm a man of my word. These things — and many more — will improve your life as a student and your life in general, no matter what kind of student you are right now.

Let's use two comparisons. If you want to be a very good athlete, how do you do that? You practice, practice, and practice. You listen to your coaches, do what they say, and practice even more. That's how you get ready for the next game.

How do you become a good musician? Same thing. You practice, you listen to your music teacher, and you practice even more. Then you're ready to play in front of an audience.

I think you can see where I'm going. If you want to be a first-rate student, you study (practice), listen to your teachers (coaches), and study (practice) even more. That's how you succeed in school. That's how the athlete wins and the musician gives a winning performance.

My book is filled with advice. I give you very clear and useful steps. I call them "Strategies" with a capital "S." You'll become the kind of student you'll be proud to be. Everyone around you will congratulate you on your accomplishments — from your teachers, to your whole family, and even to your friends.

Before we begin, let me ask you to keep this thought in mind — your education is really important. It'll determine how successful you are in a career, and even how much you enjoy life. I've talked with thousands of students over the years, and they all say the same thing: *"The more I became a better student, the more I felt great about myself."*

Robert R. Neuman, Ph.D.

Dr. Bob

Put on your climbing boots.

. . . .

There are lots of ways to think about being a student who learns new things from day to day — and from year to year. You could say it's a lot like taking a journey or constructing a building. Personally, I like to think of it as climbing a mountain: It's an adventure, and it's challenging. The view from the top is awesome.

If you want to be a great mountain climber, what do you need? Well, before you even put on your climbing boots, you have to want to do it. You have to want to get to the top. That means you have to think that what you're doing is important to you. You're setting a goal for yourself, a big one, and you'll need to be determined to succeed.

Being a student **is** just like mountain climbing. A student wants to succeed by getting high grades, by setting ever-higher goals, by liking the challenge, and by always aiming for the top. (The top is starting your life in the world, by the way.)

Also, just like a climber, when you learn, you're never alone. You'll always need directions and advice from others. It starts with your teachers. They tell you *what* to learn and *how* to learn.

Sometimes you need advice from counselors and often from your parents. They're interested in your success. As a student, you should never feel like you're on your own. Parents, teachers, and counselors are your coaches/guides on your way up the mountain. They'll help you when you need it — if you ask.

Right now you're getting advice from me, an expert who can tell you how to succeed as a **College Smart Student**. I'll give you 12 ways to become that student.

A College Smart Student will climb the mountain and reach the top — and enter the workplace prepared. Will that person be you? If so, you'll be the kind of person employers look for. **Employers report right now that young people with the traits you'll find in this book are very hard to find. Use the 12 Strategies, and you'll stand out from the crowd.** If you take my advice, I promise that you'll never regret it.

Now go get your boots and let's start climbing.

THINK ABOUT THIS:
Just like a mountain, school changes from level to level. It gets harder and harder, the higher you go. You must adjust and change tactics as you ascend, using more climbing/learning tools as things get harder.

ONE MORE THING:
Going forward in this book, you ought to highlight important points, so you can go back to each chapter and quickly review them. Highlighting is a habit you want to develop because it's a useful, time-saving learning technique.

Boot-up your mind for the 21st Century

· ·

Y ou already know how quickly everything around you changes each day. In the 21st century, your century, very important things will quickly change, like jobs, careers, and your personal life in general.

Want an example? Not long ago, your parents used big, clunky computers. Now you can carry around a computer in your backpack — or even your pocket.

What do these fast and frequent changes have to do with you as a student? They mean that you have to become an excellent learner/student to keep up with a future where change is an everyday thing.

In short, it means that you will have to be a student for the rest of your life.

Imagine yourself in a job or a career. As soon as something new comes along, you have to learn it right away. How is that different from being in class? Your teacher says, *"Okay, tomorrow, were going to move onto the next chapter in your book."*

Do you see that it's all the same? Whether it's on a job or in school, it's the same thing. Learn, learn, learn.

You're in for a lifetime of change and learning. That's why the 21st century is called the Information Age. How will you manage it? If you become an excellent learner now in school, then you'll be an excellent learner in an exciting and interesting career after college.

Remember the comparison I made earlier about becoming a winning athlete or a great musician?

When you practice, practice, practice, what's happening inside of you? The better you get, the more you will like moving on to greater things:

winning more games against tougher opponents or making great music even when the music gets harder.

Both examples are just like being a student. The harder you study, the more you'll want to study because you're ready for the new challenges that lie ahead. If you get better at what you do — learning — the more you'll want to learn. You'll feel that being a student every day means more than you ever imagined. It's a fantastic feeling!

Read these two pages a second time.

Now take a minute to highlight the important parts. It's always best to highlight on the second read. That way you know what's really important because you're already familiar with the information. If you highlight on a first read, you tend to highlight too many things.

Which Student Are You?

Learning is the key to your future — most students don't get this. Let's go back to the question I asked you earlier: How much do you like school? Or to put it another way, how do you like being a student?

In this chapter, you'll meet three types of students. Which one are you?

If you become serious about school, that's a major step. You're growing, starting to realize how important your education is to your life, and you're starting to think about where you want it to take you.

THE JOB YOU GET MAY NOT EXIST YET!

Each year of school takes you in new directions as you gain more knowledge. Middle school leads to high school, high school leads to college, and college leads to a job and the rest of your life! Did you ever stop to think that in this fast-moving century, the job you may get may not exist yet!

Wherever you are in school, what you learn this year becomes even more important than last year. It's crucial that you always take what you learn one year on to the next. (More on this later.)

So have I persuaded you to get serious about all this stuff? Okay, keep moving. I believe that every student has the potential to do awesome things.

How serious do you need to be? Well, "serious" doesn't mean you suddenly lose the fun in your life or become a different person.

SERIOUS MEANS DYNAMIC.
Think superhero. You take control of things in your life each day so you can do everything you need and want to do.

It means becoming an independent and skilled student who improves day by day. Are you with me?

DYNAMIC STUDENTS ARE GOING PLACES.

As a dynamic student, you are supposed to learn and get the highest grades you can. Each day, your grades on tests and assignments determine your final grades. Learning helps you feel good about yourself and helps you grow in self-confidence. But there's more to learning than just grades. You're saying, *What?!* More on this later.

The plain fact is that what you do every day as a student — listening with attention to your teachers in class, following directions, completing assignments, meeting deadlines, and studying with concentration — has really far-reaching effects.

What you do now as a student mirrors what you will do as an adult in the workplace: going off to work each day, getting there on time, doing a job according to someone's directions, meeting deadlines and the demands of others, and trying to succeed by using your head. These are skills that employers prize.

Right now, employers complain that young people lack these skills.
Here's the truth: School is a job where you are paid in knowledge and

grades. School gets you ready for a career. And that's your big goal. That's why getting serious is so important.

Productive people are always in high demand.

- ## Colleges want productive students.
- ## Later, employers want to offer them jobs.
- ## Good students become valued employees who go places.

School also teaches you to become a person who gets things done. All those assignments, tests, projects, lab reports, and papers teach you how to be self-motivated and active. If you have initiative and energy, employers will hire you. Later, your boss will notice these abilities in the workplace.

Take a good look around you. Look at other students in your school. Then ask yourself, *"Who will succeed in life?"* Why do you put some students in the successful category but not others?

You can tell by their everyday actions. Serious students get things done. They're going somewhere. They're moving ahead. They're better organized, and they succeed in everything — from extracurriculars to classes.

What about you? What will your friends say if they were asked if you'll be successful?

From semester to semester, from year to year, successful students are in control of themselves: focused and balanced. They see a successful and exciting future for themselves. They plan ahead. They set and reach goals because they're going places.

I'm going to show you how to go places. We're on a roll, so read on.

WHY SHOULD YOU LISTEN TO ME? FOR MORE THAN 12,000 REASONS

If you're going to believe what I say, you should believe I know what I'm talking about.

Over the years, I've advised and counseled more than 12,000 college students. I've spent more than 25 years talking one-on-one with students. I probably know more about high school and college students than anyone in the country. The Strategies in this book come from talking and working with these students —

- Students trying to keep up and on-track in classes every day
- Students struggling with grades
- Students with great ambitions
- Students who didn't get why school and learning are so important
- Students who were successful but wanted to do even more
- Students who couldn't get a handle on their small goals or life goals
- Students who were confused, but who deep down wanted to succeed

I know the problems students have and how to solve them. My Strategies have proven themselves over and over again.

WHY MY STRATEGIES (WITH A CAPITAL "S") ARE SO IMPORTANT.

As you go through my book, you may find that you already have some of my Strategies under control. That's great. Often, just knowing that you are doing the right thing in the right way can be reassuring.

Other Strategies may be new to you. Still others, you might not take too seriously until you read through them and understand their importance.

All the Strategies are important. Practicing and perfecting them every day will put you in control of your life and your courses. The Strategies will make you successful, less stressed, more confident, and focused. Most importantly, when you've mastered the Strategies, **you'll always be ready for the next challenge** from one level of school to the next — and eventually the workplace. Speaking of the workplace....

WANT TO BE RICH AND FAMOUS?

Lots of students do. Certainly, these are high goals. But if you ask these students *how* they're going to achieve this fame and fortune, they don't always know.

Let's return to our mountain-climbing comparison for a moment. If you're a student who is serious about succeeding, you need to look at the entire mountain. You should be thinking about reaching the peak and enjoying the view from the top (it's your future).

But some climbers only watch the path that's right in front of them or the rock that they're crawling over at that moment.

Want to figure out what kind of climber/student you are? After you've read all three descriptions below, check the box in front of the title that best describes you as a student now. **Be honest!** Don't worry about the three labels. You need to know who you are at this moment.

If you want to change, the Strategies will help you do that.

☐ *'Sup?*

Do you think school is something to get through and leave behind? Do you find school dull? Maybe you're waiting for the excitement to begin, but it never seems to arrive. You live in the moment.

Do you think of school in terms of compartments? You move from one course to the next, one semester to the next, one year to the next. Each is separate, and one compartment seems just like the next.

What else? You're bored. So you don't exert yourself. Your goal is to work just enough to get an okay grade, but not to do more work than you have to.

Mostly, you're satisfied with getting by. Sometimes that means getting a pretty good grade for doing not very much work. (More on this later.) Getting an occasional bad grade is okay with you.

Setting goals is not something you think about. You're willing to trust to luck or fate that things will work out.

☐ *So-So*

If you're a **So-So Student**, you probably study harder than **'Sup.** You put forth effort — but only when you want to.

You study for tests and complete assignments, but then you often draw a line: You don't work at courses that you don't like or that you find hard or too boring. In general, you earn pretty good grades, but basically, you work for grades, not to really learn.

You have no real sense of how all your classes fit together to form a whole. There's no BIG picture for you. What's more, like **'Sup,** you don't think about how your classes today prepare you for tomorrow — or even your whole life. And when someone asks you about goals, you just say, *Goals?*

☐ *College Smart*

This is what all students should be, whatever year of school they're in: what I call a **College Smart Student.** College is the high point in everyone's education, whether or not they know it. So whether you're already in college, or on your way, you need to become **college smart:** That means being at the top of your educational game.

When you're **college smart,** you know that grades are not your only goal. They're certainly important, but when you're **college smart,** you always think of the large purpose: studying and learning to build your future. (Don't worry about grades. If you're a **college smart** learner, your grades will be excellent.)

Gaining knowledge, developing learning skills, and achieving your course goals all mean that you're looking beyond classes, semesters, and grades. You're already thinking about a career after college — **that career is where your learning is going to take you.**

Even though your life goals may be a bit hazy, as a **College Smart Student,** you're always thinking ahead. For example, you might say to yourself: *"I like math. I wonder if I would like engineering or business?" "I like language and literature. I wonder if I would make a good journalist, or press secretary for someone in government?"* Look ahead. Set new and higher goals. Forward-looking students actually create many opportunities now and later in their lives. More on this later.

> *When students are college age,*
> *their brain is at its physical peak for learning.*
> *COLLEGE SMART students make the most of it.*

College Smart Students see the BIG picture. Do you have a Big Picture?

What's the Big Picture?

- Every course you take develops (exercises) your mind in a different way.
- All courses come together to form a whole. An education is not lots of compartments: separate courses, or separate semesters.
- Taking one class seriously but blowing off others narrows your mind and closes doors to your future.
- Broad knowledge gives you different kinds of opportunities in the workplace and makes you more valuable.

BEING COLLEGE SMART: YOUR KEY TO SUCCESS.

So let's agree you're going to become a **College Smart Student.** You do this by using the Strategies in this guide. As you get better at using them, you'll believe that anything is possible — you can reach goals, carry out plans, and fulfill your ambition. You'll be in control of your whole life.

Plus, you'll find that your courses become more interesting, even exciting. You can achieve high grades, learn lots, and feel the confidence that comes with great personal success.

Now that you know what kind of student you want to be — **College Smart** — let's take the first steps.

LISTEN TO DR. BOB—
To be a College Smart Student: what it takes

Your education has to be high up on your list of important things in your life.

You're the one who has to make choices about school and your future. And there's no such thing as starting too early. This is your life. So begin by knowing what kind of student you are now. Then decide what kind of student you really want to be. That's the next step in becoming **college smart**. It's what the next chapter is about. Read on!

Did you highlight the important points? Go back now and highlight information that specifically applies to you. After this, no more reminders about highlighting. We'll talk about other things.

Do you know yourself
deep down — inside and out?

LET'S EXPLORE.

This section helps you think about yourself in new ways. You are more complicated than you know! Now that you've got your climbing boots on, let's climb a little higher. Are you ready? Let's zero in on you as a student.

1. How do you value these aspects of your life? Use a scale of 1 to 5 on each. (1: least important. 5: most important.)

☐ your health   ☐ your part-time job
☐ your social life   ☐ your education
☐ your extracurriculars   ☐ your family

2. Regarding school, circle the letter that best describes you.
   a. a student who enjoys everything about school
   b. a student with strong likes and dislikes about school: teachers, courses, studying, tests
   c. a student who finds school less and less interesting year by year
   d. a student whose favorite class is lunch

3. As a student, how would you describe yourself? Circle <u>only one</u> answer.
   a. a student who earns all high grades and works to keep them high
   b. a student who earns all high grades, but doesn't work too hard for them
   c. a student with mostly high grades, but not always
   d. a student whose grades could probably use a good jump-start
   e. a student who'd rather not think too much about grades

4. If academic success and good grades are important to you, why? Rank each statement using a scale of 1 to 5. (1: least important. 5: most important.)
   ☐ You enjoy the admiration of teachers, family, and friends.
   ☐ You look forward to financial rewards later in life.
   ☐ You like earning academic awards (honors, scholarships, etc.).
   ☐ You look forward to moving to a higher level of education.

Keep these answers in mind as you read the rest of this chapter. In a few pages, you'll see what you've just learned about yourself.

KNOWING YOURSELF MAKES YOU SMARTER.

Do you understand yourself as a person? As a student? Do you think about such things? Knowing more about yourself as a person makes you smarter about everything. The better you understand yourself as a student, the better your education and your life will be. So let's get to know you better.

First, let's look at your whole life, beginning with all the roles you play as a person:

- Son/Daughter (Parents won't let you forget THAT role.)
- Brother/Sister (That's a role you might want to forget now and then.)
- Athlete (Go team!)
- Best Friend (Hey, what's going on?)
- Boyfriend/Girlfriend (Ahhhh!)
- Employee (I'll get right to it.)
- Club/Group Member (Let's do a fundraiser!)
- Musician/Artist (WOW!)
- Religious Person (Silence.)
- Computer-Game Player, TV Watcher, Social Media Fanatic, and so forth. (Vegging-out.)

Do you see that your life is filled with activities linked to all the roles you play? How do you feel about these many roles? Some, you love. Some, you don't. Some you hardly ever think about until you're asked, like now. It's important to know yourself. Think about these things regularly.

 BE COLLEGE SMART. You're a complex person, and life asks a lot of responsibility from you. Even if you weren't a student, your days and weeks would be filled with activity. Add your life as a student, and you start to wonder how you can manage it all. But it's no longer a matter of *if* you can. You have to. And you have to figure out how. College and life demand it.

YOUR EDUCATION IS A BOAT. TAKE THE WHEEL.

You're at that point in life when you can't sit back and watch life pass you by. Still, you can't just dive into life like it's a river and let it sweep you up and toss you around. Are the waters in your river rough or calm?

Once again, it's time to take control. So no matter how fast, rough, or deep the river, you can still get from one place to the next — and not just any old place, but specific destinations (goals) that you choose for yourself.

In the river of your life, you need a boat — a sturdy and reliable one. And right now, that boat is school — your education. School will get you from here to there. Can you steer the boat so it gets you where you want to go? Even on short trips? What about the long trips? Where do you want this boat to take you in your life? To get where you want to go, you have to know how to be the captain of your boat.

To be **college smart**, the skilled captain of your educational boat, you must:

- make sensible decisions
- manage your responsibilities
- organize your time
- set goals
- keep an eye on your direction
- evaluate your progress
- celebrate your achievements

That's a lot, I know. Just take a look at one of your typical days. Use the **Weekly Activity Map** that follows. Choose any school day, just one for now. Fill in each hour of your day from 7:00 a.m. to 11:00 p.m. Be accurate and honest. Take your time. Include <u>everything</u> you do.

You may find that because your activities are not neatly divided into hours, certain activities may share a box. That's okay. Just make sure they're included.

Here are some ideas to get you started. Feel free to add more. (You'll use this same list later in this chapter to fill in the entire week.)

- Put in your class hours.
- Add the hours you usually study and do homework.
- Don't forget the hours you watch TV, movies, or use social media.
- Record naps, long phone calls, or hanging out with friends.
- Don't forget hours you spend working a part-time job, practicing with your team, playing your musical instrument, going to lessons, or volunteering.
- List the times that you eat, shower, etc.

YOUR WEEKLY ACTIVITY MAP

Go to www.GetCollegeSmart.com and download a copy of this map.

	Sun	Mon	Tue	Wed	Thu	Fri	Sat
7:00							
8:00							
9:00							
10:00							
11:00							
12:00							
1:00							
2:00							
3:00							
4:00							
5:00							
6:00							

7:00						
8:00						
9:00						
10:00						
11:00	Go to Bed!	Go to Bed!	Go to Bed!	Go to Bed!	Go to Bed!	
Total						

KNOW WHERE YOUR TIME GOES...

When you've finished, you'll have a visual map of one of your busy days. Surprised by the number of things you do? Seeing all you do in a day tells you a lot about how you use your time.

For the hours that you're in school, school requires you to be in certain places — classes, labs, and so forth. If you have a job, that time is also planned for you. Are you an athlete? Better get to practice. **How many hours in your days are really yours to decide on?**

You may not know it, but your life is changing. You're taking on more responsibilities — whether or not you want to. You have to start acting differently.

When you grow out of those old kid habits, you become the captain of your boat. You begin to learn how to read maps, plot a course, navigate, and make decisions about where you want to go.

If you just let the water take you wherever it's going, you might not like the places when you get there.

...AND WHAT YOU CAN DO WITH TIME

Being a captain means you recognize that all of your life roles are important, including your student role — and you're the one who maps them out.

Yet the student role is the one that too many students treat like an annoying brother or sister. Yes, your education can be demanding, even a bother: all those different courses, teachers, study, tests, and homework assignments. But like your brother or sister, your education is not going away. It better not, because your life depends on it.

The learning skills you develop and the information you accumulate in school will help you throughout your life.

- Learners are recognized and go places. Employers are always looking for employees who can learn new jobs and do them well and independently. Being a **College Smart Student** gives you a great advantage in job interviews. (More Later.)

- Because learners are resourceful and talented, learners make great employees. They can do all kinds of things. This makes them valuable. They're the ones who get promotions.

- Learners are in demand because they're intelligent and creative, always looking for better opportunities and setting new goals. They're in demand in the marketplace during good *and* bad economies. They're thinkers who can be trusted to do the job.

- Learners live interesting personal lives as adults. You'll like learning all kinds of things, and these interests will keep you from ever being "bored."

In short, first-rate learners can do anything they need or want to do.

BE COLLEGE SMART. Right now, your job is being a student — an excellent student. How will you be paid? You're making an exciting future for yourself.

GET A HANDLE ON YOUR TIME.

If you look at your student role as a job, you have to look at a whole work week to really see what's going on. So now it's time to fill out all the days in your **Weekly Activity Map.**

Take your time. Fill in the boxes carefully, and you'll really know yourself, inside and out, top to bottom. Don't forget to fill in the weekends. You live in a 7-day week.

Directions

1. Record everything you do during a week's time. Go back to the **Map** page. Then add up the hours you spend studying each day. Enter them on the Total blank.

2. Keep this thought in mind as you continue. I want you to see that because your days are so busy, sometimes you just don't have time to think about school and study. What you have to figure out is how to put school and studying back in your day — not let the other things squeeze it out.

3. Once you've filled in your **Map,** think about this. A good college expects you to study at least 25-30 hours a week as a freshman. I think you'll agree that's a lot. The younger **College Smart Student** looks ahead to that and builds study "muscles" to get ready to be able to put in that study time. If you're in college now, you have to move fast to meet this goal. So let's work backwards.

If you're in high school now, you have to be ready for that 30-hour routine. That means you should be studying at least 20 hours a week as a high school senior, 15 hours as a junior, 10 hours as a sophomore, at least 10 hours as a freshman. **Studies show that 66% of college-bound high school seniors study no more than 6 hours a week!**

If you're already in college, you have to accelerate your pace dramatically, and that's going to take effort. As the car ads say, 0 to 60 in just seconds. Your adjustment is going to be a big change. But you can do it if you want to! Make the time to finish this book to get started with the Strategies.

Whatever year you are in school, the idea is to always study more hours this year than you did the previous year.

But let's not get ahead of ourselves. Right now, I just want you to be aware of what your days and your weeks look like. They're probably packed. And study is probably on the losing end of the activities that compete for your time.

> Even if you're an A student now, your real goal is to become a high-powered learning pro. That means you learn more about how to study better as you study more each year.

In Strategy 8, you'll use the information in your Weekly Activity Map that you've just created to plan your day and your study time. Right now, we want to just put down on paper what happens in your days. In the time it takes you to get to **Strategy 7 & 8,** start to watch where you time goes from day to day. You'll learn even more about yourself.

If you don't "learn how to learn," you'll be a student who <u>starts</u> college but:

- needs extra years to earn a degree
- loses your career dreams or
- never graduates.

Getting <u>into</u> college is the easy part. <u>Succeeding</u> in it is hard. That's why only about 1 in 3 college students graduate in four years. College covers twice as much material as high school in half the time. College students need to be skilled and efficient learners with mature study techniques to handle challenging information.

When you control your study hours — making sure they're an important priority in your life — you'll succeed in all your courses, even those courses, where you feel *"I'm just not good in that subject."*

If a subject is harder for you, you should study it more. Some subjects just need more time. We'll talk more about learning and time in **Strategies 7 and 8.** The better you study, the more you'll learn. And that takes effort, just like athletics or music. But remember: you want the rewards of being a **College Smart Student.**

FITTING IT ALL IN — IT'S UP TO YOU.

Let's put things together. The point is that knowing yourself is important:

- Are you a very good student who wants to grow into a better student?
- Are you a **So-So** student who gets great grades but you're not really learning much?
- Are you more of a **'Sup** student who needs to take better control of time?

What I want you to do right now is recognize all the roles you play in life and how they fill your day. If you want to improve as a student, you have to control not only your student role, but your other roles as well.

That's why we began by looking at a typical day for you. Your school organizes your school day. You organize your study time. Or do you? Are you the kind of student who takes control of your time? Or do you just let things happen?

The BIG QUESTION we are trying to answer is this: Do you control your week, or does it control you?

When you were filling out your **Weekly Activity Map** and realized that you would have to include homework/study time, did you start running out of time?

Do you see how we're getting closer and closer to understanding how well you know yourself as a student? You'll learn more and more as you move from one Strategy to the next.

Controlling time is a BIG DEAL. Whatever kind of student you are right now, you should know this important fact: Learning takes time, and therefore, to be a learner, you have to make time for learning. This is the key to success in college. But before you can put in the time, you have to find the time.

Sleep or die! (Well, almost!) Don't forget the importance of sleep: from 11:00 p.m. to 7:00 a.m. During these hours, you should be sleeping. The research says so.

If you don't eat right or keep your body in shape, you'll feel the consequences, but not right away. If you **don't sleep enough, you'll feel it tomorrow and for days to come. Lack of sleep is deadly** to a student. Sleep deprivation, as doctors call it, makes your mind wander and even shut down at times. Understanding or remembering what the teacher says in class becomes difficult, if not impossible.

Isn't your main job as a student to use your mind? Absolutely. So don't do anything that makes your mind weak. Sleeplessness will do just that.

About Sleep. Some people need more sleep than others. Figure it out for yourself. It's easy to do. Try this: Get a normal eight hours each night for two to three nights in a row. Then ask yourself, *"Am I tired during the first two classes of my day?"* If so, go to bed earlier for the next two to three nights. How do you feel after getting more sleep? Adjust your schedule to get the amount of sleep your body needs.

A late night here and there won't kill you. But too many will.

Don't kid yourself about playing "catch-up" with sleep by staying up late during the week and sleeping all weekend. It doesn't work.

Research also shows that whatever your habits are in middle and high school, they become more intense in college. And in college, bad sleeping habits can become much worse if you let them.

Eating healthy is important, exercising is important, but sleep is essential.

Write your own Declaration of Independence

. . . .

YOU'RE SHAPING YOUR LIFE.

When you look ahead to your future, what is it that you want? To be independent. To be yourself and to create your own future — a future that includes career, success, and personal happiness.

It all begins in school. Don't believe it? Think about it this way:

- Your teachers decide what you should learn in a class, *but you control how and when to fit studying into your days.*
- Your school tells you that you need certain requirements to graduate, *but you have to figure out how to control and succeed in all those courses every day.*
- You take a variety of courses, *but you're the one who figures out how to succeed in courses that can be very different from each other. You use your mind in different ways.*

You say these examples don't make you independent? How free do you want to be? Free like your parents? Good. Let's see how free they are.

TAKE A GOOD LOOK AT YOUR PARENTS' LIVES.

When you were young, you thought that your parents were totally free — because they were grown-ups. That's a child's perspective. Don't they also have bosses, schedules, projects, deadlines, and assignments at work every day? Doesn't that sound like school?

And then there are all of their other responsibilities, like carpools, attending your events, grocery shopping, gassing up the car, cleaning the house, taking care of the family budget, making appointments with dentists and doctors. The list goes on and on.

If you really take control of your life and manage your independence NOW, you'll understand you have responsibilities. The kinds of independent decisions you make every day in school will prepare you to succeed as a student, *and to succeed later on as an adult and in a career.* (More Later.)

So from this point on, make this declaration: "I'm the one who decides what kind of student I will be." As you move through each phase of your education, you'll say, "These are my decisions and they're good ones."

So how do you use the Strategies?

TIGHTEN UP YOUR CLIMBING BOOTS.

A Message from Dr. Bob: I'm going to coach you through each of the 12 Strategies, but before we start, I want to give you some general pointers.

As you read each Strategy, think of these six important facts.

1. The more Strategies you use, the better you'll do in school.
2. It's never too late to start. No matter where you are in school, start using these Strategies right now. Today.
3. Believe in the Strategies. They've proven themselves for years.
4. You're in charge of your education. Anytime you start a new course, say to yourself, *"I'm in control. I'm the captain of this ship, and my life depends upon it."*
5. Give school the respect it deserves. That means giving it the time it deserves. It's the pathway to your future.
6. You need to practice these Strategies every day. And like an athlete or musician, you'll get better and better.

These are the Strategies you'll find in the next part of the book.

Strategy 1 — How, exactly, to "use your head"
Strategy 2 — Your study place
Strategy 3 — The first two weeks of the semester
Strategy 4 — Knowing how to talk
Strategy 5 — Talking to your teachers
Strategy 6 — Talking with your guidance counselor
Strategy 7 — Studying vs. homework
Strategy 8 — Controlling time
Strategy 9 — All about tests
Strategy 10 — Tracking grades
Strategy 11 — Extracurricular activities and recommendations
Strategy 12 — Setting goals

You're climbing the mountain. As a person who is independent and in control, you're becoming a successful learner, prepared for life in college and in the Information Age. These Strategies will show you how.

STRATEGY 1

**How, exactly, to
"use your head" —**
(Directions included)

· ·

WARNING:
You don't just pour knowledge
into some hole in your head.

LEARN MORE ABOUT LEARNING

Okay. Use three words to complete this phrase: My mind is like a _____:

1. _____
2. _____
3. _____

When I ask students to do this, the words students usually give me tend to fit into two categories.

GROUP A	GROUP B
Box	Computer
Suitcase	Tree
Closet	Engine

Do you see that one group thinks of their minds simply as containers? The other group sees their minds in a more complex way, working and dynamic, and in the case of the tree: a growing thing. You want to be in Group B.

Group A students. They have container words for their minds. They think learning is something that just happens to them. If they sit in class, the teacher will pour the information into a hole in their head. No sweat.

Group B students. College Smart Students, on the other hand, think of their minds as processors, working instruments, busy centers that transport information, living things that grow, or use energy to produce results. These students know that learning takes time and organization. They know what their job is, and they get it done. And that's because they know how their mind really works. For these students, being in school is active, exciting, and rewarding.

LEARNING TAKES ENERGY. LEARNING IS ACTIVE.

Walk into a classroom, sit down, and class begins. The teacher says, *"Today we're going to begin studying the US Constitution"* or *"Today we'll learn how to calculate the molecular weight of a chemical compound."*

Processing minds learn in layers. Let's look at these layers of learning.

- **Layer 1:** Before you step into the classroom, you're already familiar with the class material because you've read ahead.
- **Layer 2:** The teacher is really *reviewing* for you what you've already read, so the class means more to you. You focus on the teacher's words, stay on-task, and take meaningful notes.
- **Layer 3:** You can follow what the teacher is saying — it's not completely new. You're also able to take better notes because you have background on the topic. You may find you develop your own system of quick writing. (If you're not yet a good note-taker and can't keep up with the teacher, ask if you can record the class. Always ask permission.)
- **Layer 4:** You're ready to ask good questions. You can contribute to class discussions.
- **Layer 5:** Later, when you sit down to study and rewrite your class notes, you're reviewing what you've learned — strengthening your knowledge even more. Everything begins falling into place and making sense. Plus, this isn't the last time you go over this material. You do it frequently during the time you're studying it.

You're gaining knowledge layer by layer. Layered knowledge stays with you. It "lasts." And it all begins with working ahead of the next class.

CONTAINER-HEADS JUST SIT THERE WAITING TO BE FILLED.

If you're a container-head, you don't work ahead in class. You walk into class with a mind that's blank. You may find it hard to keep up with what the teacher is saying. You don't have any questions to ask, so you don't contribute to class. Maybe your mind wanders.

You just hope that when you walk out of class you've learned something. Then, when it comes to taking a test, you complain: *"I didn't think that was going to be on the test. I didn't really get what all that was about."*

Container-minded students sit in class thinking that the teacher is just going to pour knowledge into their brains. Students imagine they have a funnel inserted into their heads. Then the teacher simply pours a lot of liquid/knowledge from the bottle into the funnel.

But the funnel has only a small opening, so half the liquid/knowledge ends up on the floor in puddles around the students' feet. Container-heads take very little knowledge with them. The puddles are still on the floor when they leave the classroom.

HOW TO *REALLY* LEARN WHILE IN CLASS

- Read ahead so you're familiar with the topic.
- As a result, you feel more confident in class.
- The class becomes a review of what you've already read.
- You take better notes and ask about anything you didn't understand when you read the chapter.
- When you study after class, everything falls into place. You work on assignments, review/rewrite your class notes, and study more to make sure everything "sticks."

If you don't put in the effort, you won't learn. (Don't be fooled by good grades. You might still get good grades if you're a good crammer, but the information won't stick.). It's as simple as that. If your mind isn't in "receiving and processing mode," most knowledge just spills on the floor.

BE COLLEGE SMART. Most students frustrated by their grades believe their minds are containers. They depend on the teacher to pour facts, formulas, etc. into their heads. What's more, these students expect the teacher to process that knowledge for them in class, much like happened in grade school. Not anymore. The teacher uses class time to present and explain and to answer questions. Learning is the student's responsibility.

ONCE AGAIN, YOU'RE IN CONTROL.

Once you understand that learning is processing information, you will adjust the way you think. *"My mind is not a container. It's an organism, an engine, or a computer that constantly needs care and activity (thinking, learning) to stay healthy or well-maintained."* When you absorb, organize, process knowledge, and use it, you're learning. It takes time, but you're in control. It's the way to develop the learning skills you need for college and, certainly later, in the workplace.

And what you learn will stay with you — because your mind will develop and grow along with the knowledge and information you absorb.

So decide right now. Is your mind a box or an engine? a jar or a machine?

Once the students I worked with understood that the mind is a knowledge processor, they began telling me —

- *"It sounds dumb to say it now, but the fact that learning takes time each day and week was a real discovery for me."*
- *"Yes, I thought the teacher was supposed to "put" things in my head. When I began to think of my mind as a computer processor that I controlled, my grades went up immediately."*
- *"Whenever I start a new class, I say to myself, 'I'm going to really nail this class.' I can do it if I don't think about how hard the teacher is or how many books I have to read. I just focus on how I'm going to manage this new subject day by day."*
- *"If I get an A in a course, I say to myself, 'I handled that. WOW! Good for me.' If I get a low grade, I say, 'I'm still acting like a kid in grade school.'"*

Turn on your metal processor as you read the rest of this book!

LISTEN TO DR. BOB
Why you need to practice this Strategy for College

If you are used to getting most of your knowledge during class, you'll be out of luck in college. Start now to practice learning on your own. Earning high grades in college is much, much tougher than you've ever experienced. The majority of college students learn this the hard way. They expect college to be the same-old, same-old. They couldn't be more wrong.

You're about to meet Andrea. This is the first in a number of stories that will show college students in typical real-life situations. These are not stories that happen occasionally. I chose these stories because they are situations that are happening right now all over the country. Andrea represents thousands of students in her predicament.

After talking to students one-on-one for 25 years, I became an expert on the problems that defeat college students. That's why I wrote this book. I'm using my insights to help you avoid these mistakes. The 12 Strategies will guide you.

UP CLOSE AND PERSONAL

Andrea: The Earlier the Better

Andrea was clearly unhappy, discouraged, and depressed. I talked with her after a clearly disastrous first semester in college. Her GPA was bad news even though she had graduated with honors from a good high school.

The first thing I discovered about her was that she didn't spend nearly enough time studying. She agreed, *"Okay, more time studying."*

At the end of the second semester, she saw me again. Her grades hadn't gone up very much at all. "What do I do now? What am I doing wrong?" she asked. With her grades, she was hanging on by her fingernails.

She was afraid to go home for the summer to face her parents.

"What if I get kicked out of college? What if I have to go back home for good? Mom will go bonkers. My dad will give me pamphlets about joining the army. Green is just not my color, and I've never gotten up 'at dawn' in my life."

When she returned to the start of her sophomore year she had new determination. We agreed that she needed to look at college study from all angles. Andrea knew she had to make some big changes.

Dr. Bob: Okay, you've been studying more; you went from 10 hours a week to 20. This semester you want to be up to 25-30.

Andrea: That's like a full time job!

Dr. Bob: Now let's look at HOW you study.

She took a notebook out of her backpack.

Dr. Bob: Where do you study?

Andrea: In my dorm room.

Dr. Bob: That's too distracting. Find new study places.

Andrea: Where?

Dr. Bob: How about the library? Lots of quiet, out-of-the way corners there. Dorms have study rooms; and I know the Union has study areas. But find a quiet one, not a social one.

Andrea: Right. In fact, the dorm next to mine has a basement study area.

She was taking lots of notes.

Dr. Bob: Andrea, when do you study?"

Andrea: All the time.

Dr. Bob: No you don't. Do you study at 3:00 a.m.?

Andrea: Sometimes — especially if I have a test the next day.

I put my head in my hands.

Andrea: Did I say something wrong? Do you have a headache, Dr. Neuman?

Dr. Bob: No, but I'm on the way to one. Andrea, now take some very careful notes for yourself.

> #1: I'm going to get out of my dorm room. It's too distracting.

> #2: I'll make a daily and weekly **Map**, AND STICK TO IT.

> #3 I'll increase my study time to 30 hours each week, studying regularly for each course and keeping up with them all.

> #4 I will take time to eat and sleep.

> #5 When I follow a map without turning my days upside down, I'll be studying better.

> #6 Studying is like playing an instrument – the more I practice, the better I'll get.

Andrea: Maybe I can learn to play the banjo! That was just a little joke, Dr. Neuman. You're supposed to laugh.

Dr. Neuman: Hah!

Andrea: I get it, I get it! Studying is a process, and unless I find the steps to the process, I'll just stay stuck in neutral, and my grades will stay the same.

Dr. Bob: No. In fact, if you stay in neutral they'll probably go down because your courses are getting harder.

I had hardly finished my sentence and Andrea was up from her chair, backpack on her shoulder, and shaking my hand. *"Dr. Neuman, I'm going to do it!"*

And do it she did. The next semester she showed me her grades. She had them enlarged to poster size at a print shop on campus, and she now could look at them on her dorm wall. Every day they reminded her that she was moving in the right direction.

At the time I talked with Andrea, I hadn't yet written my book, but she, and thousands like her, let me see where and how real-life students need help with all kinds of problems. The 12 Strategies grew out of our work together during these conferences. The Strategies are the real-deal. That's why you're reading this book right now.

Andrea didn't become a **straight-*A*** student right away, but after two more semesters, she was on a roll. By her senior year, her grade point average was 3.50. She became a **College Smart Student,** maybe a little late, but she did it. Graduation was a real celebration! Her dad and mom were ecstatic. And the US Army just had to get along without her!

DEAN'S COMMENTARY

Andrea is like too many students who think that they can approach college work casually with an *"It'll-all-work-out"* attitude. Nothing happens that way. Andrea needed very practical and specific advice on how to become a **College Smart Student.** In the end, it all worked out for her. She took control, set goals for herself, and felt great for her efforts.

Remember the learning mountain? Always aim for the top. As you move higher, the work gets harder. You need to meet each challenge by studying not only more, but studying better. That's exactly why your ability to learn *has to* grow from class to class and year to year. Always be asking yourself, "How can I be a better student?" There's always more to learn, and that's what all my Strategies are about.

STRATEGY 2

**YOUR STUDY PLACE—
Quiet, Comfortable,
and Maybe You Even
Feng Shui-ed It *(look it up)***

A good study place is a valuable tool you use to manage your time, control your days, and learn better. This is your personal place where you get things done as a student.

LEARN MORE ABOUT YOURSELF

Check all that apply.

When I study —

☐ I like to sprawl out on my bed or the floor.

☐ I study at a desk.

☐ I study wherever I can, here and there, makes no difference.

☐ I study in different places every day for variety.

☐ I study in my room because that's where my music and the computer are.

☐ I like to study near a television and my phone because I like the distraction.

☐ My study area is private, quiet, and comfortable.

☐ My study area is respected by other people around me.

If you're *really* going to learn — retain knowledge, not cram — and get high grades, you have to study. The first step in developing good study habits is having a great place to study. It should be a place of your own, a place that is quiet and comfortable, away from noise and commotion.

BE COLLEGE SMART. This idea is important, and so it's worth repeating. Study in a place that gives you the best results for the time you spend studying. Be efficient in your work. It gains you time.

HOW GOOD IS YOUR STUDY PLACE?

You would not normally like to sleep on a hard floor, or eat while running, or watch a movie with people talking over the dialogue or blocking the screen. It's the same with learning. Your study place should be well-chosen, well-located, well-organized, and comfortable. Let's face it: Studying is work. It requires concentration. It's true! Try it! As you learn to study better, you'll study more. The more you study, the more you'll enjoy it. The easier it gets. It all begins with a good study place.

Here's a checklist for you. Check the items that describe your study place.

☐ A quiet place, away from other activities and distractions

☐ A BIG ENOUGH desk or table

☐ A bright desk lamp

☐ A place to keep a set of learning tools — everything from monitors to highlighters

☐ A comfortable chair — your body, as well as your mind, has to get into the learning mode

PUT ON YOUR STUDY CLOTHES

Believe it or not, students have told me that they actually have "study clothes" — everything from their worn-out jeans to their grubby sweatshirt to their favorite cap. So maybe you want to try it. Say to yourself: "Not only do I want to study in places where I can concentrate, I want to be comfortable in what I'm wearing." Comfort and concentration go hand in hand.

Besides comfort, clothes can be a signal. They warn anyone who might drop by your study area. "When I'm wearing my study cap, please stay away. I don't want to be disturbed unless the building is on fire."

PRIVACY EQUALS PRODUCTIVITY.

A Smart Phone™ is really amazing. It's a notebook, a photo album, a music library, and a way of texting your friends.

But when you're trying to study, a Smart Phone becomes a tremendous distraction. Leaving it on all the time interrupts your concentration. The result? Either studying will take much longer than it should, or these distractions can prevent you from learning much at all.

So whenever you say to yourself, "I'm studying now," turn off all your electronic devices. You'll get more done in less time. When you study, you have to take a break from your social life. When you've finished studying, you can return to your Smart Phone world. If you're on your computer, make sure you're logged off of your social media sites. No, you're not cutting yourself off from your friends when you study; you're only separating yourself from them for a little while.

HOW ABOUT MUSIC?

To study and learn really effectively, music in the background or in your ear will distract you. Most **College Smart Students.** find that they do their best studying in a quiet place. But if you find you need background sound, play some music that pleases your ear without distracting your mind. Try meditation music — it's non-distracting, a relaxing sound. So be moderate in your need for background sounds.

Why? Because if you stop to think about it, there are different intensities of study. Some study is easier, like arranging and rewriting class notes. Other study, like working on difficult math problems or writing the first draft of an essay, is much harder and may require quiet.

And as much as music distracts, using the TV as background noise makes studying nearly impossible. Your attention is completely divided. This is no way to become a **College Smart Student.**

PORTABLE QUIET

If finding quiet is really difficult, you might want to invest in a pair of soft earplugs found at drugstores. They become portable quiet devices: Keep them handy whenever the general commotion is just too distracting. You might even find that earplugs are your answer to a good night's sleep.

GET IT TOGETHER.

You can be the most organized, the most serious, and the most determined student in the world. But if you don't have a good study place, you undercut all those wonderful qualities.

When you are studying and learning, the PLEASE DO NOT DISTURB sign should be hanging in a place for everyone to see. When you have your own private and personal study place, you can control the quality and quantity of studying that you know you need.

And remember: studying and learning are your responsibility. When you take the time to create a place all your own, you accomplish great things, the kind of things anyone would expect from a **College Smart Student** like you.

Now go back to the LEARN ABOUT YOURSELF that began this Strategy and compare your answers to what you've learned. Do you need to work on your study place? That's okay. It's a step in the right direction. Every time you use a Strategy, you're helping yourself to become an excellent student!

LISTEN TO DR. BOB —
Start learning the value of a good study place right now. Choosing and using a good study place means that you're taking a major step toward taking control of your life and working toward your personal success.

UP CLOSE AND PERSONAL

Kirsten: What do I tell them? Balancing social time and study time

If you were to meet Kirsten today and ask her about college, she would probably say: "My big problem in college was friends, they were just too friendly."

What a thing to say! That's what friends are for: fun, enjoyment, hanging out, closeness, friends forever. The big problem, especially for a serious student like Kirsten, was that her friends had to be close to her even when they weren't. So every time they had the urge, which was constantly, they had to phone her, or text her, or send her a new picture, or tell her they had pizza for lunch — with pineapple.

Because she was such a good friend, Kirsten was like a mom to her friends. "Kirsten, what do I do if Cory wants to take me to homecoming?" "There's a sale on at Sachs. Want to go?" etc.

I told Kirsten I would help her though her problems, but she should do most of the thinking.

Kirsten: I don't want my friends to be mad at me.

Dr. Bob: If they're really good friends, they'll still like you, even if you tell them not to contact you during your study time.

Kirsten: But how will they know?

Dr. Bob: Give them a copy of your **Personal Map.** *(More on this in Strategy 8.)*

Kirsten: Right. That will even help me follow my **Map** more closely. But they have so many ways to call me.

Dr. Bob: Kirsten, I know it may seem like removing one of your kidneys, but YOU HAVE TO UNPLUG.

Kirsten: Right. I'll turn off my phone. No texting —that will be more like removing my right arm.

Dr. Bob: You might even pull out your music earplugs when you study, and put in plugs that block sound. You can buy them at a drugstore.

Kirsten: Do I have to? Really? Dr. Neuman, you're a real slave driver!

Dr. Bob: You'll get used to being "unplugged." I'll bet you study better without these distractions. Can you really memorize a list of 50 terms with rhythms beating through your head?

Kirsten: All right, I'm going to sit my friends down this weekend before the game, hand a copy of my **Map** to each one, and say, "If you want me as a friend, let me be a student."

DEAN'S COMMENTARY

Kirsten loved her friends, and she wanted to "love" college just as much. No one can get along without friends; no one should have to.

But life, especially school, requires setting priorities and maintaining balance. Kirsten learned how to do both. She told her friends that studying was at the top of her priority list; but they were up there, too. By giving a good **Map** (**Strategy 8**) to her friends, she could keep her priorities AND balance things in her life – for her, two of the most important!

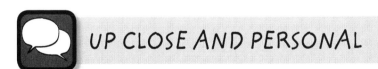

UP CLOSE AND PERSONAL

Ethan: Roommates — You gotta luv 'em.

Like Kirsten, Ethan had a "people problem." In his case, the person was his roommate. They liked each other, even though they had different interests. His roommate was sports nuts. If there was a game on TV, he was watching it with his lucky Packers cap. Ethan liked sports, too, but for him that meant mainly games on campus: football, basketball, even hockey. Ethan played club volleyball.

So it wasn't their interests that were the problem. It was that his roommate was always in his bed watching Sports Network. And several of his friends were usually there, too.

That meant Ethan had to go someplace else to study. That was not too bad. He had what he called his favorite peaceful *study holes* around campus. But the problem got more serious when Ethan's roomie watched sports all evening, and then studied late into the night. That's when Ethan preferred to sleep – something his "mate" did during the day.

Finally, Ethan declared a TIME OUT.

Ethan: You know you're my favorite roommate.

Roommate: Like, I'm your only roommate, dude.

Ethan: Just let me continue. Unlike you, I need to do things more, let's say, normally.

Roommate: You saying I'm abnormal?

Ethan: Just hold on for a minute. I like to study during the day, sometimes right here in our room. And I like to sleep usually between midnight and my 8:00 a.m. class.

Roommate: Like, dude, why would anyone want a class, like, at dawn?

Ethan took a deep breath.

Ethan: ... so are you following me? See how different we are? We're both spending a ton of money on college. So, for me, college is more important than the next Nicks' game. Ethan stopped talking, and smiled at his roomie with sort of a pleading expression. Ethan didn't know it, but his request fit right into his roomie's way of thinking.

Roommate: Right, right. I totally see where you're coming from. How about we do this? We'll divide things. Let's work it out like on a score board. Each week, I'll put my games on the schedule; you put down your in-house study time.

> If you want to study here during a game, I go to someone else's room. If I want the guys to come here, you get lost – or I mean, study elsewhere.

> And we can call the hours from midnight to whenever (you know I usually sleep 'til my first class at noon), as time-out-on-the-field, or half-time. You'll have quiet. Okay?

> Great, dude; gimme five. I gotta get back to the game, I think half-time's over. With a hand slap, Ethan and his roommate were on schedule, one game (or week) at a time.

DEAN'S COMMENTARY

How were Kirsten's and Ethan's problem similar? They both had challenges involving friends, time, and the priority of school. Friends and roommates sometimes need to be handled like your pet dog. They live close to you, their enjoyable, but you have to work with them on their manners. When you say "study," they should respect that and go someplace else. When you say, "quiet," they should give you alone-time. And like your dog, they will love you and enjoy your company all the more because they know their limits and will work around your needs. Just as you will work around theirs.

So when it's time for you to study, sleep, and do things for just yourself, you can say, *"don't bark!"*

STRATEGY 3

The first two weeks —
*What you should do while other
students are waiting around
for something to happen.*

· ·

The semester is beginning. Maybe it's even a
new year getting started. You've got some new
teachers and a new class schedule. This is when
controlling your courses starts, and organization is
the name of the game. Are you ready? Let's go!

LEARN ABOUT YOURSELF

When a new semester begins, what should you do to start it off right? To get you thinking, assign each statement below a number from 5, most important, to 1, least important.

☐   Make a notebook for each course.

☐   Look through all your textbooks.

☐   Get a calendar and jot down important dates for each course.

☐   Look over course outlines, and pay attention to grading policies, tests, major assignments, and deadlines.

☐   Introduce yourself to each new teacher by asking a good question.

In your opinion, why do you get low grades in some courses? Again, score these answers 1 to 5.

☐   Difficult tests.

☐   Difficult teacher.

☐   The subject is difficult.

☐   Too many other things to do this semester.

☐   Too many other difficult courses.

☐   The competition from other students is too tough.

☐   The subject is not interesting.

EACH SEMESTER IS A NEW BEGINNING.

Every new semester gives you new opportunities. A new semester means you're moving one more level up that learning mountain. Courses are more challenging for you, and that means your life as a student is more demanding. If it's not, something's wrong.

Even if a new semester seems like the "same old, same old" — and even if you have an *A* average — you still need to set new goals for yourself to become a more skilled learner.

Starting a new semester with new plans is the best way to grow as a student. You'll have even more control of your education, your study habits, and, of course, your grades. Like climbing that mountain, you're looking upward and moving upward knowing a lot more about what's to come.

So, what should you do to start a new school term? Completely review the last semester, preferably with your counselor or adviser.

These are the items you should cover:

- What grades did you earn last semester?
- Were you satisfied with them?
- Were they consistently high, or were they irregular?
- If you got lower grades than the semester before, do you know why?
- How many hours did you study each day and each week?
- Did you **Map** out your study time?
- What were the main things that got in the way of getting high grades?
- What do you have to change in this new semester?
- How do you plan to make those changes?

Now that you've reviewed these things, how are you going to dive into the first two weeks? That's what this strategy is all about.

HOW TO LOOK AT THE FIRST TWO WEEKS

At the start of each new semester, most students don't do a lot of planning, thinking, or organizing.

If it's the start of a new year, they get caught up in a flurry of other activities — everything from hugging their friends that they haven't seen for a while, always good to do, to comparing class schedules and teachers.

Then they look at their new course schedule. Will the work it requires interfere with their own "personal schedule?!"

Most students don't get down to business right away because they haven't been in the "school groove" for awhile. Sort of like returning to your old workout schedule when you've been just lying around.

Before they know it, these late-starting students find themselves facing the first tests in each class. The early weeks have just disappeared. Where did the time go? **The grades on those first tests, BAD NEWS.**

Semester after semester, students are caught off-guard by first tests. This is an all-too-familiar pattern. Why? Many students just don't have a good sense of controlling their time. These students will say a variety of things:

- "Nothing much really happens in any course in the first two to four weeks."
- "I don't really know how much I need to study until I start getting grades back. If I start getting low grades, I'll try to study more."
- "If my grades are 'high enough.' I know I'm all right doing what I'm doing."

BE COLLEGE SMART. As important as the end of a semester is, the best students I've known tell me that they concentrate on the first two weeks. Getting off to a strong start makes their courses easier, especially in more difficult courses.

SHOW UP AND COME TO PLAY.

Have you ever heard anyone say, "That team lost the game in the first ten minutes"? What does that mean? Usually two things: The team didn't come to the game in shape or ready to play. And the team did not size up the opposition very well. So what should you do the first two weeks of the semester?

Come to the classroom ready to study on the very first day. Listen to the briefing your coach (teacher) gives you. At the beginning of any semester, the teacher spends time talking about the course, course materials, and what he or she expects of students. The teacher also goes through a course outline to let the class know when major assignments are due and when tests are scheduled, along with how much each counts toward the final grade. **Pay attention to this information. It will tell you —**

- how much material will be covered during the semester
- what the teacher expects students to do — and when

The course outline shows you how to size up the course. It gives you an overview of the entire semester. It lists the tasks to be completed in this course and when they will occur. You'll be looking at the scope and pace of the reading assignments as well as the milestones that will determine your final grade. You'll see the amount of work involved in this course. As you'll learn later, this information gives you the power to control the course.

WHERE YOUR STRESS REALLY COMES FROM

Remember **So-So** and **'Sup**? They don't listen to any of this very well because they think *they've heard it all before. They're waiting for something to happen.* There's plenty happening. They just don't realize it.

> Generally speaking, students who use their time during the first two weeks of a course to think and plan do the best at the end of the course.

The way to decrease your stress? Get a headstart on the semester. Be focused, energetic, and active during the first two weeks. Because **So-So** and **'Sup** don't get started until something pressures them to do so, they're always playing "catch up."

Most students spend the first two weeks taking it easy. Many think they are saving their energy for when things *really get going*, later in the semester. What they don't realize is that their slow start to the semester actually increases their stress later on.

9 WAYS TO START THE SEMESTER SMART

When you get off to a strong start in the first two weeks of the semester, you're much like the team that "comes ready to play." You're getting yourself in shape and sizing up your classes.

Here are nine basic steps that will get you ready to play. Make sure you do each one!

1. *Evaluate your success last semester.*

Most students walk out of final exams and close the door on those classes. With a sigh of relief, students say to themselves, "That's over." They don't have to think about those classes anymore. Right? Wrong.

If you're really on-top-of-it, you'll learn something about yourself from each class. Right away, after that last test.

- What did you do that helped you succeed in the class? **Remind yourself of what worked and try to build on that strategy in the future.**
- What did you do that hurt your success, put you behind, or cost you points on a test? **Resolve that you won't make those same mistakes next semester.**

2. *List your good habits*

What kinds of good habits are you looking for? Here are a few examples.

- Following a weekly map. (More later in **Strategy 8.**)
- Recopying your class notes and textbook notes each night, reviewing them, highlighting important points, and adding comments.
- Completing reading assignments and keeping up with the course outline.
- Rereading each chapter to improve your understanding of the material.

- Talking to your teachers after tests are returned to see how you could've improved your grade.
- Making lists or flashcards of things that have to be memorized.
- Creating outlines or charts or other study tools to summarize course material.
- Keeping a calendar of tests and due dates and working ahead.

3. *List your bad habits*

What kind of bad habits got in the way of your success? Here are a few common problems that students wrestle with.

- Studying just now and then, haphazardly.
- Putting off assignments until the last minute.
- Taking poor class notes.
- Coming to class unprepared.
- Not paying attention in class.
- Cramming for tests at the last minute.
- Not writing enough drafts of papers.
- Not rereading course material.
- Missing deadlines and being penalized.
- Not asking questions to clarify assignments early on.
- Not talking to teachers and keeping track of the progress (grades).

You might even make a chart of your good and bad habits. Put it in your daily planner or the inside covers of your subject notebooks. Read it often as a reminder of what you should and shouldn't be doing to succeed.

One more thing: talk to your teachers about grades that surprised you on tests. Those conversations are always helpful.

Talking to a teacher about grades is <u>not</u> a complaining session. And it shouldn't be. Teachers don't give low grades because they don't like you or because they're having a bad day. When it comes to grades, teachers have two main goals: to be accurate and to be consistent. You're going to the teacher *to learn what you did wrong and try to improve,* not to argue a grade.

4. *In the first couple days of the semester, slowly page through all the books and materials used in the course.*

Be familiar with the whole package from the start. It's like planning your climb on the mountain: know where you're going, how you're going get to the summit, and how to prevent mis-steps along the way. Learn as much as you can about this "climb" (semester) before you start.

5. *Read all the information a teacher hands out at the beginning of the semester.*

These course outlines, directions, summaries, and grading policies are your teacher's way of emphasizing that this is what's going to happen in the course. These materials tell what's expected of you: to win the game you have to be familiar with the plays.

Highlight or underline the important points. **File this material somewhere safe, so you can go back to it anytime throughout the semester.** Review it often. It will keep you focused and in control of the course. **You'll always know what's going on and what's coming up.**

If you have questions on any of these important details, see the teacher right away.

6. *Use a monthly calendar to map out what's going on in all your courses.*

Buy a planner or use the planner on your computer. The important thing here is **to see the entire month at a glance.**

Using your course outlines, jot down dates in your planner for all tests and major assignments throughout the semester. Now your calendar gives you a bird's-eye view of everything that's happening. Your master calendar shows you what's going on in ALL your courses. Update as needed.

Because your calendar gives you an overview of the whole semester, your calendar alerts you to weeks with heavy loads and warns you when tests and assignments are just around the corner.

You now have the advantage of looking ahead. Students who don't know one week what's going on next week always get into trouble. They fool themselves into thinking that there's not much to do this week. **That's because they don't know what's due next week!** Keep on top of your courses by knowing what's coming up.

7. *Before two weeks have gone by, have one private conversation with the teacher.*

You have to get over the idea that talking to teachers is uncool or just a way to get higher grades. **College Smart Students** tell me that talking with teachers gives them a better comfort level in all classes, even in the hardest classes. Why? Talking to each teacher fact to face (person to person), makes you feel more at ease.

Most teachers really enjoy talking to students outside of class. Here are some possible topics:

-   Talk about what interests you in this course.
-   Let the teacher know if this is a new subject for you, or...
-   If you're finding the course difficult... or
-   How this course relates to other courses you're taking.

 If you should find yourself slipping in the course, talking to a teacher you already know is a whole lot easier than talking with a teacher you've never spoken to before. (You'll find more about talking to teachers in STRATEGY 5.)

8. *Schedule a time to see your assigned counselor/adviser.*

These knowledgeable people give you personal guidance. Stay in touch with them throughout the semester. They can help you with all kinds of issues. Check in with them regularly: two times a semester if you're doing fine; once a month if you're having problems.

What do you talk about? Anything that's affecting your success in your classes. If you think about all the Strategies in this book, any one or more of them are worth reviewing. Take the book in with you. Reporting regularly to your counselor keeps you on track. (More about this in **Strategy 6.**)

9. *Make a chart for your grades.*

Yes, each teacher has your grades in a grade book, but you should look at your grades often to track your progress. True you got an *A* on the first test of the semester, but remember: courses get harder as they go on. And so tests are going to get harder. Tracking your grades lets you know where you really stand. (More on this in **Strategy 10**.)

NEED HELP? DON'T DELAY.

As you're climbing your mountain, you run into something, like a rock slide, that keeps you from moving ahead. Now what? You pause and think about what to do. Well, maybe you can figure it out yourself. But probably the best thing to do is to consult your main guide (your counselor/adviser or the teacher).

The same is true in school. You begin a new course, and within a few days, you're dragging behind the class. Or you begin a new section in a course, and suddenly, you're really confused. Or maybe it's the start of a new semester, and you quickly know that you don't have all your courses under control. In these cases, you need the expert help of your teacher and your counselor/adviser.

Don't hesitate, and don't be embarrassed — you'll avoid some horrible situations.

Whether it is consulting your teachers privately or scheduling appointments with your counselor/adviser, DO IT. Be college smart enough to get out in front of your problems early while they still can be solved.

Think of it this way. You get sick; you don't get better; you don't go to the doctor. Finally, you're so sick that you see the doctor who says, "Gee, I wish you'd come in earlier. We could have fixed this right away in a week. Now it's going to take month."

Learning how and when to get help is a personal skill. It's one that you learn in school and it'll serve you well for the rest of your life — in a job and in life in general.

Asking for advice is a trait of every successful person. And that includes you!

LET'S TEST WHAT YOU'VE LEARNED SO FAR.

What would you do in each one of the situations listed below? (To fill in the blanks, either test your memory on what you've read so far in this Strategy or go back over the Strategy and find the points you want to list.)

Difficult tests

_____

_____

Difficult teacher

_____

_____

Subject is difficult for you

_____

_____

Too many other things to do

_____

_____

Too many other difficult courses

_____

_____

The competition is too tough

_____

_____

LISTEN TO DR. BOB —
Why you need to practice this Strategy for college
Remember: In college, you do twice the work in half the time. You have to be ready and figure out how you're going to pace yourself. Be pro-active, not reactive. You want to be in charge of your work, the captain of your ship. If you're not getting an overview of what's entailed in your classes and transferring the "grade-able" items to a calendar, you're not looking ahead. You have to look ahead to control things. If your calendar tells you that you have an out-of-town track meet in three weeks, and a paper is due the day you return, what are you going to do about it?

UP CLOSE AND PERSONAL

Chad: Oui, oui! This is French — new subjects always take more time.

Chad had two years of Spanish in high school, but he was tired of Spanish and wanted to take a new language to fulfill his college foreign-language requirement. Chad chose French. His girlfriend in high school had taken French, and she had liked it. Besides, Chad thought it might be cool to be able to go to French restaurants and order wine with an accent.

Day One in French 001: Chad finds himself a seat in the back of the room, and the instructor comes in speaking to the class in French. Chad looks around and sees many, but not all, students nodding with understanding.

Day Two: Chad realizes that the days of high school foreign language are long gone, and his instructor is moving at a good clip. Many of the students in this class have already had one or two years of high school French. Chad thinks to himself, "This is going to be hard." He slips further behind with each class.

Week Four: Chad is getting a *D* in French, passing by the skin of his teeth. Finally, the professor writes "please see me" on Chad's quiz. (It's an unusual request. Typically, professors don't ask to see students. Students are supposed to do the asking.) Chad talks to his professor, who recommends that Chad get a tutor. Chad takes the advice because he doesn't know what else to do.

Two days later: Chad meets with a French major, a senior, whom he likes a lot. He sees the tutor regularly. Chad's lucky. The university's language department provides tutoring as a free service. At another university, Chad might have had to pay the tutor an hourly rate.

Week Seven: No question about it, the tutor has helped. Chad's quiz grades have improved, and Chad earns a *C* on the midterm test.

For the rest of the semester, he meets faithfully with his tutor. By the end of the semester, he has earned himself a solid *C* in the course.

At first, Chad is greatly relieved. But then he realizes he has three more semesters of college French to go! He has to continue building on his weak background in French 001. He asks himself, "Is this the way it's going to be for three more semesters? Will the amount of time I spend with my tutor increase as the class gets more difficult? I'm deep in it!"

Chad's alternative is to chalk up French 001 as a learning experience and sign up for Spanish 001 second semester, which he does. **But Chad paid a price that affected more than his French course.**

In struggling to save his French grade, he robbed time from his other courses, so all of his grades suffered. Chad's *C* in French wasn't the only *C* he got. **In his first semester in college, his grade point average was already low.**

⤴ DEAN'S COMMENTARY

In the early days of the semester, Chad did what he always did in difficult situations: He hoped somehow things would turn out okay. Chad had never worked much in high school for grades. But now he was in college. And he wasn't very college smart. He didn't study very hard or put in the extra hours he needed to keep up with his subjects, not even French.

Chad should have talked to his instructor or adviser after the first two or three days of the course. Either probably would have seen that Chad was not ready for Spanish 3. But they would have advised him to transfer to Spanish 001, **which he could *still do* early in the semester.** Spanish 001 is where his two years of high school Spanish would have placed him.

But because Chad didn't talk to anyone in the first two weeks, **he didn't know any of this.** Later, in other Strategies, we'll talk about the importance of talking. So he muddled on.

Other students in the class who had no French background did very well. But they understood that they had to study and put in extra effort. Chad just didn't want to and didn't know how. And he didn't ask for help until it was too late for an easy solution.

Sure, learning French at a college pace was going to be more difficult than building on his background of high school Spanish, which wasn't all that good. But he could have succeeded in French by improving his study effort.

True, the good news is that Chad's tutor helped Chad hobble along and pass the course. But the bad news is that Chad used the tutor as a crutch, never really getting the idea that he still was not shouldering the responsibility for his own learning. The tutor created the outside-of-class learning experience that Chad could have — and should have — created for himself by studying more and putting in more effort.

But Chad's problem is far from over: Chad is typical of so many students who must take courses in sequence: like chemistry, math, and foreign language. French 002, 003, and 004 follow French 001. When you get behind in one course, it affects not only this semester but the next semester, and the semester after that.

Chad abandoned French because he didn't want to struggle with French for more semesters, but in doing so, he paid for a French course that won't count toward his graduation. **He is also already a semester behind in his language requirement, so he will have to pay for another course and take it somewhere along the line. He's behind, and it's only his first semester of college!**

Getting behind is deadly. It forces students to change their majors, their degree programs, and their career plans. It creates stress and that awful feeling of always playing "catch-up." Not controlling courses costs you time: It can add extra semesters, and therefore extra cost, to earning a degree. And it all happens because some students never learned how to start a semester, assign enough study time to each course, and **get off to a strong and immediate start.**

So jump-start ALL your courses every semester. Start studying on DAY ONE. Organize your time and your study strategies, look frequently at your calendar (more on that later), and always be ahead of the game. If you think you're having trouble, see your teacher or counselor right away. You can never win the game of catch-up without paying the price somehow. What did Chad do? He hoped for a miracle. That never works.

UP CLOSE AND PERSONAL

Meredith: The battle of biology: retreat or advance?

As a first-semester college freshman, Meredith chose biology to fulfill a degree requirement. It was her favorite subject in high school. She didn't like chem. or physics: too much math — ugh!

She thought college biology would be like high school biology. But she soon discovered that she was surrounded by biology majors. She didn't read the course description carefully: her first mistake.

Her second? Meredith approached her college course the way she approached all of her courses — gradually. She blew off the first couple weeks.

And because she didn't read the course outline carefully the first day of class, she was shocked to learn from another student that the first test was scheduled for Week Four. And here she was in Week Three, totally unprepared.

The day of the test, she couldn't answer the first multiple-choice question, and by the time she reached question 50, she was sick to her stomach asking herself, "What do I do? Do I drop this course? I don't think that I can drop it. It's a requirement. I'm really messed up." Her grade was a **D.**

Still, Meredith was determined, so she decided to try to turn her biology grade around. I told her that I thought she might recover, but this was her dilemma: She was going to have *to make up* for the studying she'd lost in the first three weeks of biology. At the same time, she was going to have *to keep up* with each day's new material. It was going to mean lots of study time.

There was another complication. The extra time Meredith spent on biology *took study time away from her other four courses.* She was going to have to risk low grades in her other courses to save biology. What's more, I was pretty sure Meredith was in much the same situation in her other courses: Behind! She had realized too late what she should have been doing during the first weeks of the semester. But she couldn't turn back the clock.

So Meredith dropped biology and devoted that extra study time she gained without biology to her other courses. The result was pretty good grades in her remaining courses. Her GPA was 2.7. But she had a *W* grade (showing she had **W**ithdrawn from biology) on her record. That grade was a wake-up call for Meredith, and she was smart enough to hear it. Never again did she "take it easy" at the beginning of a semester.

Meredith learned a lot from one mistake. She admitted it was all her fault, and so she turned her college life around 180 degrees.

⟲ DEAN'S COMMENTARY

Studying a course is like constructing a building. You build it one day at a time, one level at a time. You start with the foundation. A strong foundation creates a building that will last for years. However, if the foundation isn't strong, there is no solid base. The whole building teeters. So it is with learning: When you neglect your studies early in a course, you've weakened the foundation for the rest of the course. The course, like a building, is likely to crumble and fall.

So remember the comparison between building and studying and say to yourself at the start of each semester: "I won't get behind in any of my courses! I'll always keep in mind that as a **College Smart Student,** learning takes work, determination, and intelligence. I can do it, but it's all up to me!"

And always keep in mind that as a **College Smart Student,** your "job of learning" is no different than the work that a serious athlete brings to a sport or the effort that a musician spends working with an instrument. To win the game or make great music takes time. And that time begins on "day one."

STRATEGY 4

Knowing how to talk —
*it's more than running
up the phone bill*

· ·

The best students know how to talk. They're
good conversationalists. Good questioners
and explainers. They are at ease talking, and
they express themselves clearly — in class
or out. They do more than simply repeat
the latest clichés: "It was, I mean, like, so
totally cool, so awesome, you know."

Students who talk well are usually noticed, liked, and remembered. Why? Because what they say is usually interesting or adds to the quality of the conversation. Good talkers never fall into the category of "just another person." Frequently, they are leaders: They captain sports teams, hold offices in student government, and organize special school projects. These students understand that by talking, they can make things happen. Successful adults are good talkers. Talking well is a big deal.

 ## LEARN ABOUT YOURSELF

Check each one that applies to you.

- ☐ I'm comfortable talking with my friends.

- ☐ If I have a choice to talk or not, I prefer not to.

- ☐ I talk seriously with my parents.

- ☐ I can easily talk to my friends' parents, even when my friends aren't around.

- ☐ I get easily flustered when I have to speak to people other than my close friends.

- ☐ I can talk to adults in general — in stores, the library, other public places — and not be self-conscious or stumble through what I have to say.

- ☐ I get really nervous talking to teachers and counselors/advisers.

When students are able to talk well with anyone, anywhere, this skill adds to their maturity, self-confidence, independence, and personality.

College Smart Students are good talkers. So, always remember that talking well really separates excellent students from all others. "Talkers" know how to use words to express themselves clearly and concisely in all situations, whether in class or out.

BE COLLEGE SMART. If you can speak to adults without using ums, you knows, and likes ... if you can say yes rather than yeah to adults ... if you can look adults in the eye when you talk, you'll set yourself apart from others.

HOW TALKING MAKES THINGS HAPPEN.

Talking is the primary way we exchange ideas, information, and feelings. If you stop to think about it, your days are filled with spoken words. If you added up the number of words that you read, write, and speak in a lifetime, spoken words would vastly outnumber words that are written or read.

Talking makes things happen. When you talk, you explain things, you answer questions, you get people interested or excited about your ideas. You get yourself recognized. Ask any adult, "Who gets the highest raise or the promotion?" Usually, it's the people who know how to talk.

Non-talkers or poor talkers might hold jobs, but they often don't go anywhere in a career. Generally, talkers are the people who know how to best communicate what their business does. In one way or another, every job involves explaining something to others, clearly reporting results, or giving directions. Talkers earn reputations as valuable contributors. Talkers are leaders. In many instances, skilled talkers are considered indispensable.

You can have all the knowledge and great ideas in the world, but.... if you can't get your thoughts out into the world — expressing them by talking clearly and persuasively — they will remain hidden. That's why talking is so important. It determines, to a great extent, what you do, who you are, and who you will become.

As I use the word, "talking" in this Strategy, it doesn't simply mean saying words, like "Pass the ketchup, please." We all do that. We have to, just to get through our day-to-day lives. Talking, in the most complete sense of the word, means drawing on a well-developed vocabulary and organizing the words to convey thoughts that are often complicated or complex.

Talking well requires thinking and organizing thoughts on the spot. Now that takes talent. You have to practice this talent to develop it.

Talking also involves careful listening. How can you respond to people intelligently unless you understand what they're saying? Good talkers typically really listen to others. You rarely hear good talkers say, "I don't remember the teacher saying that" or "I didn't know that was going to be on the test."

Talking in class. (What's really going on here?) The next time you're in a classroom, take a good look at what's happening there. A teacher is talking to students about a subject. In fact, the teacher often does most of the talking. But when the class is asked questions, which students talk the most? Usually, it's the best students who are responding to or asking questions. Why?

These students know that talking helps them understand their own thoughts. In other words, talking keeps their minds working. Remember the difference between students who think of their minds as containers and those who think of their minds as processors? Good talkers are always processors.

Since talkers are involved in their courses, the material becomes more interesting to them. And because talkers usually have something intelligent or thought-provoking to say, they make the discussion more interesting for others. Talking relies on give-and-take: exchanging ideas.

Classes should be social experiences where students feel excited because they're working with each other toward a particular goal — learning the subject. It's why some students will say, *This class is really cool.* Students leave these kinds of classes feeling that learning is exciting because the teacher is excited about teaching, and other students are excited about learning. They want to "talk" about it. **Talking makes classes interesting. Talking's at the heart of learning.**

> *Your education is not just about getting the right answers on test questions. Your education should include developing communication skills.*

One way to develop those skills? Talk in the classroom: Answer the teacher's questions, ask your own, and join in the discussion. You should talk in all of your classes, not just classes you like. At first it may take courage, but then it will become easy. As you'll learn later in **Strategy 5**, talking in the classroom directly prepares you for a career, later on: talking with people, exchanging ideas, working together. But remember this: You have to practice both in-class *and out* to become a good talker.

TALKING GIVES YOU PERSONAL POWER AND CONFIDENCE

- Talking puts your thoughts into words.
- When you choose good words and link them together, listeners can better understand your thoughts and ideas.
- Talking sharpens your mind. It makes you think faster "on your feet."
- Talking well means you pull your thoughts together <u>before</u> you actually speak, not <u>while</u> you're speaking.
- Talking also helps you become a better writer. Good writing is talking on the page, but with more formality.

Talkers you don't need. Some students talk all the time in class — they talk to each other, but not about the subject. Their behavior is rude and distracting to the teacher and the students around them. These students don't care about learning, at least for the moment. Then, they don't do well in the class, and they blame everything else but themselves. Complaining is their favorite kind of talking.

"Talkie" students love to recruit others to join their group and fool around. You need to keep a safe distance. They'll make it hard for you to concentrate.

HOW TO PRACTICE TALKING

Talk with people of different ages. Any student can talk with friends about day-to-day stuff. However, **College Smart Students** can talk well not only with their friends, but also with —

Teachers	Grandparents	Doctors
Employers	Neighbors	Dentists
Parents	Salespeople	Coaches
Friends' parents	Young children	Senior citizens

Talk with your friends about different topics. It's good practice, and it's a place to start. Be mindful of carrying on a good conversation without adding your "usual" phrases throughout. Also collect your thoughts before you start to speak to see if you can avoid the "ums." It will be hard at first, but keep at it. Spend some time talking about topics like these:

- Why you liked a certain movie or book
- Why your sports team won a certain game
- Your personal interests/activities, like computers, music, cars, or fashions
- A story in the national news
- Something unusual in a course
- Your plans, hopes, and dreams
- Something about school (that isn't complaining or critical)
- About what kind of career you'd like after college

Talk to adults and learn about careers. Talk to your adult neighbors — and, yes, your parents and their friends. If your mother's best friend is an accountant, a career that interests you, you've got a perfect topic of conversation. Talk to her seriously about what she does. Begin by asking a question. As you listen to her, see if her job description fits what you think an accountant does.

Ask about the personal traits needed to be an accountant. Does she like being an accountant? What are the best things about the job? The worst? What advice would she give you based on her experience? You're creating a conversation. The conversation will sharpen your talking and listening skills. You'll also learn a thing or two that might encourage or discourage you about this career path.**Look people in the eye when you talk.** Don't look away or at the floor. Let them know you're talking to them. They're important listeners.

BE COLLEGE SMART. Talking well builds your mind just like working-out builds muscle on an athlete. Even if you have a long way to go to become a good talker, practice is the only way to help you steadily improve.

There are lots of words out there for a reason. They all express different shades of meaning. Look at all the words you could use to describe the idea of *moving*: run, gallop, rush, dart, jog, scamper, sprint, trot, walk, or amble. Here's another example of why you need to know about shades of meaning: being *tenacious* is thought to be a good quality, but being *obstinate* is not. One word praises and the other criticizes. Yet both meanings are related. You get the idea. To use the knowledge you have learned, you have to be able to communicate it to others clearly. A good vocabulary helps you do that directly, without stumbling around. As I said earlier, a good vocabulary empowers you and gives you confidence.

Use sticky notes with new words you really want to remember. Stick'em all over your place!

Work on developing your vocabulary! Pay attention to unfamiliar words. Look them up and write them down. Look at them regularly and try to use them. You'll be surprised how many new words you've "collected," and how useful they are.

Use an electronic dictionary and thesaurus whenever you study. It takes a little time to look up words, but it's a good way to broaden your vocabulary. Some people buy calendars that teach them a new word each day. Not a bad idea.

Being in command of a large vocabulary helps you achieve not only in college, but in a complicated and competitive world. Learning one new word each day can make a huge difference. You'll need to express complex ideas and understand shades of meaning.

TALKING YOUR WAY INTO YOUR FUTURE

What do you want for yourself in the future? Talking is the primary way you express who you are, what you think, how you think, and what you want to achieve in your life. Talking is the greatest expression of *you* — your personality, your character, and your intelligence. In all areas of life, being a good talker always gives you an advantage.

LISTEN TO DR. BOB —
Why you need to practice this Strategy for college
Talking in a college classroom is essential to learning. And it can affect your final grade.

- Can you participate in class and talk with the intelligence expected in a college classroom?
- Are your listening skills sharp enough to understand your professor's presentations, called lectures?
- Can you follow and join in the class discussions so that you say something insightful?

- Do you talk well enough to give a college-level presentation in front of a class?
- When your college course outline states that 20% of your final grade depends on class participation, will you be able to handle that?

Talking becomes important in day-to-day ways in college, too. Remember: **You're the one who takes care of yourself.** Talking well and easily will help you get things done.

- Not on the class list for chemistry? You may have to go to some office to clear up the problem. Can you do that?
- Are you signing up for a major or changing your major? Schedule an appointment with your adviser to discuss this important matter.
- You're having a health problem. You need to make an appointment at the campus health center. Can you describe the problem clearly and in detail?
- Your ID card won't scan. Find out where to go to see about it. Go straighten it out.
- Your roommate is driving you crazy! This is a major personal problem. Better sit down and talk it out, either with your roommate or your dorm adviser.
- Having trouble with math? You can't just go into your instructor's office and say, "I don't get it." To get help, you have to be more specific and explain your problem as well as you can.

In all of these instances — and a hundred more I can think of — you have to be able to talk well to handle yourself. Find the words. Be clear. Be organized in your expression. Be persuasive if you have to plead your case. You can't do that if you can't look people in the eyes while you talk and make yourself understood.

Words, words, words. At a very basic level, that's what your education and learning is about. So never leave words behind you. Besides taking part in intelligent conversations with other intelligent people, make sure you read books like novels or books about your favorite sports or interests. Read newspapers and magazines. All these activities expand your vocabulary. Words! You need them. Where would you be without them?

You're also almost halfway through the Strategies. Keep going. You're building skills that will shape your future. Process them and then practice your talking by telling someone about them!

 UP CLOSE AND PERSONAL

Sara and college interviews

Sara was used to being right. Sara was super-intelligent, and as a high school senior, she had a 4.0 grade point average and a perfect score of 36 on her ACT. She could have done the work at any of the handful of really top colleges in the country. Many would have probably offered her significant scholarships. But when it came to talking, Sara couldn't carry on a conversation with adults. She would stammer and mumble and look at her feet.

In her junior year, she applied to the best colleges in the nation. All the schools set up interviews with her in the fall of her senior year. Top colleges want to talk with students who apply for admission. These colleges also want to see memorable teacher recommendations. Prestigious institutions can afford to be picky about the students they enroll.

During interviews, admissions counselors want to talk with applicants to measure their personal qualities. These colleges want interesting students who can express themselves as well as earn good grades and scores.

Sara simply blew all her interviews. She never made it past the interview stage of any of her applications to top schools.

Her teachers could say, "Sara is a very capable student," but they couldn't say anything else.

Our university did not require interviews and accepted Sara. She ended up in a literature course with – guess who? Me.

When I read her first exam I was blown away. Why wasn't this student talking in class? So I asked that she make an appointment to see me. I was very blunt: "Sara, what is going on with you. Your exam was one of the best I've ever read. Why don't you share your knowledge with the rest of the class by contributing to discussions?"

No one had ever talked to Sara like that. Others just said, "Sara is just a quiet person."

She almost started to cry, but instead pulled herself up and said, "I don't know what's wrong with me."

"Sara, I'll tell you what's wrong with you. Nothing! You have a great mind, and I suspect that hidden somewhere behind your wall of silence is a person who has great things ahead of her. But how can you accomplish great things?"

I didn't have to answer my own question. Sara sat up in her chair and said, "I have to learn how to talk. How do I do that?"

So I gave her some "homework."

1. Talk to each of your professors during their office hours.
2. Tell them that you're learning to be more expressive and comfortable talking.
3. Ask if you could come in now and then to just have a conversation about class.
4. Go to the Counseling Center and talk with a psychologist about "shyness."
5. That person will give you some exercises to do. DO THEM!

6.   Go online and type in "Shy in College." I know you'll learn a lot.

As a dean, I could keep an eye on all Sara's classes and grades. I could tell just in my class that she was emerging from her shell. In class, she made one comment the first week, two the second, and by the end of the course she was a whole new student. She waved to me at graduation, and I could see from the gold medal and ribbon around her neck that she was graduating with highest honors.

⤺ DEAN'S COMMENTARY

Of all the Strategies in this book that define a **College Smart Student,** this one is the most often overlooked. Why? Because all students think that they can talk. They do it all the time with their friends. But that's a different kind of talking altogether.

I mean whether or not you can talk more formally: to people who are important, and to many different types of adults in many different circumstances. Not being able to talk hurts all students. But the damage is not confined to school.

The quiet and shy people eliminate themselves from many jobs and careers. Valued employees —

- express themselves well
- explain their ideas clearly
- speak up in a meeting
- speak well in front of a group without stumbling
- can find the right words and get to the point right away

Most jobs depend on committees, departments, or teams working together to solve problems or come up with new ideas. Will you be able to do that?

Good talkers are prized in the workplace. Employers are looking for them right now. And they're not finding many. Be dynamic in reaching your talking goal by admitting that something is seriously wrong and be determined to change. I use Sara's story here because in spite of her great promise and her perfect ACT scores, her inability to talk hurt her. Think about the way you speak now. Will it affect you, too?

STRATEGY 5

Talking to teachers —*Just like talking to your coach*

If school were a sport, your teacher would be your coach. In fact, your teacher IS your coach in and out of class. He or she explains the details of the game (the subject) and can help you build the talents you need to play (study skills). Your academic coach also evaluates you during practices (how well you're doing in class) and analyzes your game performance (your tests). How do you get the most out of your teachers/coaches? Read on.

 # LEARN ABOUT YOURSELF

Check all that apply to you.

I talk to teachers—

☐ when I don't understand something in class or in the textbook.

☐ when I need help preparing for a test.

☐ whenever I think I can argue for more points on a test.

☐ when I'm in some sort of grade trouble

☐ when a teacher starts a conversation with me.

☐ never. Not under any circumstances.

☐ whenever the opportunity arises.

Check the answer(s) that best describe(s) your attitude:
I view talking to teachers as —

☐ really not cool.

☐ a sign of trying to manipulate the teacher to get a better grade.

☐ something that might leave me open to criticism from friends.

☐ a neutral action — it's not a big deal.

☐ a natural part of my school day.

☐ a way to help me learn more and better.

☐ a terrifying experience

TEACHERS ARE ACADEMIC COACHES

This Strategy started out by comparing a teacher to an athletic coach. It's a good comparison in a couple of ways: You're not the only one on the team (your class), and your coach directs all the players on the team. Coaching will advance you in any sport. If you make the effort to build a good relationship with your teacher, you can really improve. That's because your teacher's comments are aimed at you *individually*. **It's talk that is focused on you, your needs, and your interests.** So if you understand what it takes to be a great athlete, you should understand how to be a great student.

CLASS SHOULD BE EXCITING, LIKE THE MOVIES

When you leave a movie with your friends, what happens? You talk about the movie — what you liked and didn't like. Even if you didn't like the movie, you talk about why.

It's the same with class. *If you've been involved in class discussion,* your mind doesn't just shut off when the class is over. Did you have unanswered questions? Did some point not make sense? Did you wonder about something you just learned? Do you disagree with something the teacher said?

Talk to the teacher as you would talk to your movie-going friends. Your teacher is always interested in what you have to say. "I really like this." Or "I can't see the point of that." Or "What did you mean when you said…?" When your teacher answers these questions, you'll likely find that you like the course a lot more. And even if you don't, you've still formed an important relationship. More about that in **Strategy 11**.

When you talk to teachers about class, things become more real, more interesting, and more memorable. You're exploring ideas out loud. When that happens, you'll do better in class. You'll read chapters more carefully and take your assignments more seriously. Talking with teachers is one of the keys to a great learning experience.

SOME REASONS TO TALK TO TEACHERS

Here are some thoughts about talking with your teacher.

- **Filling the gaps.** Every student has them. Talk about those not-so-clear things you only "sort of "know *before* they appear on a test. Know this: When you don't understand one thing, you won't understand the thing that comes next.
- **Feeling good about yourself.** Are you already a regular talker in class? Talking to teachers outside of class fills your need to know more, and you'll feel good about yourself.
- **Getting answers to all your questions.** Think about those questions you want to ask in class, but you don't because the class has to keep moving. Write down your questions, and then go see the teacher outside of class.
- **Reviewing your tests.** When you get a test back, you can see what you did wrong. But then you ask yourself, "Why did I get those wrong?" Your teacher can tell you why privately. What's more, the teacher can give you pointers about how to avoid repeating these mistakes in the future. As you have more and more conversations with teachers about tests, you'll become a better test-taker. (More about this is in **Strategy 9**.)

GET RID OF ANY OBSTACLES BETWEEN YOU AND YOUR TEACHERS.

Obstacle #1. It's up to you to make the first move. You have to approach your teachers. You have to take the initiative. The first time you approach a teacher, you might have to use some courage. But do it. It's gets easier and easier. Why don't all students want a one-on-one relationship? Obstacles #2 and #3 sometimes get in the way.

Obstacle #2. Cool conduct. '**Sups** may say talking with teachers is un-cool. Well, a lot of important things in life may seem to be to be un-cool at first, like going for help when you need it. But don't adults go to specialists all the time: accountants, auto technicians, electricians, psychologists, *etc.* They get help when they need it. Do what you think is right in your relationship with your teachers. Don't worry about what the '**Sups** think. You're stronger than that because you have a larger purpose. Whatever it takes to be a good student, do it. If they're your friends, it's only teasing.

Obstacle #3. Not at-ease talking. Do you find it difficult talking with any adults, including your teachers? Can you find words, or do you stammer and stumble? Think of it this way. Adults, including your parents, of course, are interested in talking to you and finding out what's going on in your life. You're also interested in them. So they're interesting, you're interesting, so start talking. You'll get better with practice.

Teachers like talking. That's one of the reasons that they're teachers. They like to share what they know with students. They want to get students interested in the subject. But all that doesn't end when the class does. So don't say to yourself, "I didn't understand that last part. Now what do I do?" Of course you know what to do. You talk with the teacher after class. And why? Because teachers like talking with students.

PLAYING SOCCER IN CLASS

What happens when you participate in class discussions — asking questions, answering questions, making good points? The answer: You're more involved in the class, and the subject becomes more interesting and stimulating. Time flies.

What actually happens when you get involved in a class discussion? You're no longer just a spectator. A good discussion is a little like playing soccer. However, instead of a ball, you're kicking ideas around, back and forth. Express your opinion and you're kicking the ball in one direction. Challenge someone else's opinion, and you're aiming in another direction. Then, who knows? You might kick that ball/idea down the field and into the goal. Feel great? You'll feel the same way in class when you make a super point.

So remember the difference between watching a soccer game and being a player. You'll leave classes, saying "*That class really flew by.*" That's because you were involved. Those who weren't were bored.

Keep this picture in mind and you'll always be the kind of student who gets applause from the stands. Remember the layers of learning? Talking in class is one of them. And if you start talking in class, you'll encourage others to do the same. Then things will get even more interesting..

TALKING IS AN IMPORTANT LIFE SKILL.

Everything you feel and think, want or need, understand or question in life depends on your ability to talk. Talking in class and talking with teachers are exercises that will prepare you for building personal relationships, succeeding in college, and getting a job you really like.

Many profs include class participation in assigning grades. So don't underestimate the importance of being a really good talker. If you learn how to talk in class, you're also learning how to control your life in general. You'll be able to take charge of your ideas and express yourself in all kinds of situations. And that's a great feeling. Be college smart. Start now!

You need to be a good talker in a career. Most jobs depend on talking and working together with other people to solve problems or come up with new ideas. Those jobs depend on being able to talk clearly and directly about your ideas. School prepares you for this. So whether it's in school or on a job, talking is going to get you to where you want to go.

TO RECAP

Talk to teachers in and outside of class. It helps you approach learning from several different directions. The more directions, the better.

Talk in class. Ask questions and contribute to class discussion. You have plenty of opportunities to speak in class — if you take the chance!

Talk with your teachers after class just as you would talk to an adult about a movie you just saw.

Make an appointment to talk in private. Introduce yourself to your teacher. Schedule a face to face conversation early on in the semester. Once you've had the first conversation, talking to this teacher becomes easier and easier. You'll find that the course will get more interesting to you as you get to know the teacher better.

Talk when you need help. If you're struggling in a class, get help. And do it right away. Don't wait! Your teacher will help you manage a subject, get through rough spots, and suggest other things to make your life easier. But you have to take the first step.

Don't forget e-mail and voicemail. If you're having a hard time connecting with a teacher, write an e-mail, or leave a voicemail. It may not be as personal as talking, but if you need a quick answer, either option will do the trick.

 As you finish reading each Strategy, think about ways you can put its ideas to work right now, while these pages are fresh in your mind. Take action, and take action right away! Choose a teacher, and go talk about one of the topics in this Strategy.

LISTEN TO DR. BOB —
Why you need to practice this Strategy for college

Some college classes are large. Don't let that put you off. It doesn't make a difference how large the class may be. Be brave and speak up. Maybe start out with asking a question. Talking in class will get easier and easier, even in large groups. You'll be practicing for later in life.

Talk to professors outside of class, too. They're always waiting for interested students to come and talk with them right after class or during their office hours.

UP CLOSE AND PERSONAL

Jeff starts to talk and finds a career.

A student's life can change very quickly. That's what happened with Jeff, who was a very good but rather quiet student. His high school teachers liked him, and Jeff worked hard and wanted to succeed in college.

When he graduated from high school and it came time to choose a program of courses to study in college, he didn't know where to begin. His parents wanted him to pursue a very practical college major, like business administration. They thought a degree in business would give their son lots of jobs to choose from after college.

Since Jeff had never had any conversations with teachers or counselors about what to study in college, he let his parents be his guide.

Having been accepted by a business program of a nearby university, Jeff went off to college. He adjusted rather easily. He was soon taking accounting, finance, and marketing courses. For his degree, he also needed to take a social science course. He chose psychology because, even though he had never told anyone, he had always been interested in psychology: Why people do what they do, and why they feel the way they feel.

From the first day of his psychology course, Jeff's life began to change. He was enthusiastic about everything he heard in class and everything he read. He couldn't get enough of it. He was the first to volunteer comments in class and the first to answer the questions of his professor. He had never been so active in a class before. He even began to see the relationship between psychology and business.

Business is about selling and buying. If businesses understood the psychology of consumers — why people buy — these businesses could better figure out what products people wanted and how to sell these items.

His enthusiasm for his psychology course was apparent in everything he did as a student. Being excited about one course made him more interested in his other courses. It was like having a wonderfully contagious disease that infected everything he touched. Intellectually, he had never felt more alive. He quickly went from a rather quiet person to a student who was expressive and conversational.

But the best was yet to come. He decided to major in psychology and minor in business, which meant his main area of study would be psychology and his second area of study would be business. In order to do that, he had to transfer from one academic area to another. At a university, it's called changing colleges. That's when I first met Jeff. I had to give him permission to enter our college.

He told me about his new academic interest, and his extraordinary excitement was apparent. I told him to talk with his psychology professor about officially changing his program of study. He saw me again in a few weeks. When he had spoken with her, the professor had told Jeff how much she appreciated his contributions to class discussions. She encouraged him to continue taking psychology courses and even invited him to come back and talk with her as his courses and plans developed.

In a very short time, Jeff and his professor became good friends. She eventually helped him choose a particular area of psychology for graduate study as well as several universities to apply to. She wrote one of his letters of recommendation for graduate school.

I saw Jeff at graduation, and he told me where he was going to do his graduate study, and how happy he was that his academic life had become so exciting. I told him that it was all because he had followed his personal interests and started to "talk" about them. That's where students always find success, enjoyment, and satisfaction.

DEAN'S COMMENTARY

Was it Jeff's excitement about psychology that made him an eager conversationalist? Or was it his newfound confidence in his ability to talk that made him feel so great about psychology? No matter. It all came together, and it was his professor's personal interest in him that made it all work.

Talking counts, and the sooner you start doing it, the better off you'll be, as a student and as a person. So the next time you sit quietly in the back of a classroom, wondering what you're doing there, think of Jeff. Move to the front of the room tomorrow, start asking and answering questions, and go talk to your teacher. Like Jeff, you may discover your life.

UP CLOSE AND PERSONAL

Tracy: Talking is more than making noise and saying the latest cool phrases. Prepare for your future

Everyone knows someone like Tracy. Maybe she's like you. She's "so totally, um, popular, like, um, you know?" All the words within the quote marks are the current language of young people. Have you noticed that the word *very* no longer exists? It's been replaced by "so totally" at the time of this writing. Now we use *so* — as in "he's so not with it." Today's "young speak" is peppered with "ums," "you knows," "likes," and so forth. When Tracy came to see me about a problem she was having, she couldn't really describe why she was there.

True, all decades have their own jargon for young people, and this jargon changes. The words above may have gone out style by the time you read this. But there is a time and place for it: Usually, that means young people talking with others their own age in casual conversation. Are you at ease speaking to people out of your age group?

DEAN'S COMMENTARY

This is such an important point. I'm going to repeat it. I said it to Tracy, and I'll say it to you.

- Can you speak with adults?
- Can you speak to authority figures?
- Can you speak with elderly neighbors, young children, salespeople, dentists, your counselor and your professors/teachers?

- Are you prepared to speak in the workplace?

You'll need to speak in a different language. Can you do it now? If you can't, start practicing. Who will care?

- **The people who conduct employment interviews:** They're looking for poised, confident people who are thinkers and problem solvers, who seem to *have it together* — not someone stumbling and struggling to find words.
- **Your coworkers:** Can you make yourself clearly understood? Are you confident enough to ask questions when you don't understand? Are your questions clear and to the point? Can you contribute to a discussion? Work is becoming more and more collaborative.
- **The people "above you" in the workplace:** Can you express the good ideas you may have? Then you get recognized, become valuable, and get in line to move up the ladder.
- **People in the world:** You have to know how to talk. It's one of the most important skills in life. Talking is key to most of your interactions with family, jobs, and dealing with all kinds of people:
  - ◊ from the phone tech who wants you to describe your problem in detail
  - ◊ to the computer expert you've hired to do a complicated project
  - ◊ to the banker who needs information about your hacked credit card
  - ◊ to the doctor who wants you to describe your symptoms.

Your unclear information will produce unwanted results.

All of these people want easy-to-understand, organized information. You've got to find the right words and string them together so they make sense. Your listeners will appreciate it. If you can't, you frustrate them and yourself.

ONE MORE TIME

Talking is a life skill. Everything you feel and think, want or need, understand or question in life depends on your ability to talk.

Talking is a way to get noticed — or even hired — in the workplace. Can you grab onto a project or problem, analyze it and then discuss the merits of different approaches or solutions?

Talking can advance you. Those who actively involve themselves in a daily learning process and who can express themselves clearly are going places.

The rest of the employees will sit and listen, maybe take notes — sort of what the non-talkers do in class right now.

STRATEGY 6

Talking with your counselor/ adviser —*Talking it through and getting it right*

. . . .

As a student, you have so many things to do and think about. At times, it seems like your life is just one big ball of questions, uncertainties, and confusion. Well, the truth is whether you're a student or not, life is complicated. You have to sort things out and get advice, get answers to your questions, and make good decisions.

65

Think about where you're going in school. It's a day-to-day process. You have to get ready for class tomorrow. You have to prepare for a test next week. But it goes even further than that. Are you thinking about your future? Do you have a plan for college? And what about after college? And a career?

You probably have questions like these: Why are you in school anyway? Are personal matters complicating your life as a student? Do you have problems that are hard to explain? Your counselor/adviser will help you. Everyone, especially students, need advice and guidance — not just occasionally, but regularly.

 ## LEARN ABOUT YOURSELF

Check all that apply to you.

How do you relate to counselors/advisers?

☐ I think they're mainly for students having problems in classes.

☐ I see mine once or twice each semester to discuss everything from grades to the next stage of my life as a student.

☐ When I see mine, I don't know what to say.

☐ My counselor/adviser doesn't really say much to me, so my appointments are short.

☐ I make sure to see him or her when I need some forms signed.

☐ Mine is always helpful, and the Counseling/Advising Office has good reference materials and programs.

☐ What's a counselor/adviser, anyway?

ADVICE? WHO NEEDS IT?

Having been involved in college counseling programs for many years, I could never understand why students didn't want to talk to counselors or advisers. They are the very people who can help students do everything — from getting better grades to making plans for the future.

I always thought that some students are just too nervous to talk about their studies. Other students just don't want to bother. For some, it is a combination of both. But there's another explanation. It's even more basic. And I didn't really understand it until a certain student simply refused to take my advice about seeing his counselor regarding a couple of important issues. It was then that I learned *why* he kept putting it off.

He told me he didn't want to be seen in the Counseling Office because his friends thought that place was for "losers." According to him, "The only students who go to that office are the ones in trouble." He couldn't have been more mistaken.

Your counselor/adviser is one of your best learning resources and problem solvers. Yet students still consider seeing these experts as something of a nuisance or a sign of weakness. They argue...

- *"Who has the time? What will I talk about?"* True, exchanging ideas does take time, but it's another way to practice your talking skills. As for topics of conversation, there are hundreds. You'll find some at the end of this Strategy.
- *"Who needs it? I do fine on my own. Needing advice is a sign that I don't know what I'm doing."* That's wrong. Take my word for it! Just the opposite is true, as the next section explains.

WATCH A COUNSELOR/ADVISER AT WORK

Let me tell you about Katie. She was overscheduled. Her sophomore year, she was on the swim team as well as working part-time. She wasn't getting enough sleep, and she got sick. What started as a bad cold turned into pneumonia. She missed lots of school and tests. She fell behind in her homework in all of her courses. She turned to her adviser for help.

Once the counselor found out about her problems, he contacted all of Katie's teachers and explained her situation. He worked with them to plan ways that she could keep up with her assignments even though she wasn't going to class, he rearranged due dates, and he helped her finish out the semester. He solved Katie's problems and reduced her stress. And she didn't have to drop classes.

Counselors/advisers can accomplish many things for you — including acting as your representative when you need one. They understand how things work, so they can easily get things done that would be hard for you to do on your own.

But counselors/advisers help you in all kinds of ways. Generally speaking, people who make the best decisions make them after getting advice from experts. Adults go to professionals—from their bankers to their doctors for specialized advice. That's because intelligent adults value expert information. As a student, **so should you.**

To improve your life, get into the habit of consulting people in-the-know: experts and professionals. One of those people is your counselor/adviser. He/she will listen to you, understand what you're saying, *even when you don't,* and give you straightforward advice.

Here's something else you should understand: You might think that your life is filled with problems, yet even when you fix just one part of your school life, all parts of your life improve. When that happens, you'll feel better than ever — something that's hard to do in the complicated life as a student.

YOUR PERSONAL GUIDE, TOO

Because counselors/advisers have talked with so many students over a long time, they can offer you study tips or help you when you're simply going through a hard time. And having a hard time means not only having difficulty with one or two courses. It can mean getting through those hard times when you feel burned-out or when you're frustrated because you don't know where you're going.

To figure things out, counselors and advisers ask questions about your personal, as well as your school, life. The two are always interconnected.

- Some students have family or health problems that are very private.
- Some don't want to admit that school is not at the top of their "to-do" list because they have so many *other* things to do.
- Others worry that counselors/advisers won't keep conversations confidential. They will. Like all professionals who give personal advice, they have to.

So be honest with your counselor/adviser. Talk about everything that affects your education and your plans for the future. It's the kind of two-way communication that will solve your problems, and once again your life will become easier and you'll feel great.

COUNSELORS/ADVISERS ARE GOOD SOURCES OF INFO: SOME EXAMPLES.

Use the following blanks to make a list of any special concerns that you have right now. Then make an appointment with your counselor/adviser. Forget about what your friends do. This is your education, and you're going to make the best of it with the best advice you can get. List your special concerns here:

_____

_____

_____

_____

Finally, your counselors/advisers do lots of other things. For example, they can organize group discussions of interest to all kinds of students.

Are you planning to go study abroad? Your college counselor/adviser can help you. Do you want to become a teacher, doctor, or scientist, etc.? You'll need special advice. Are you uncertain about selecting a major, a job, or career?

College counseling/advising offices have programs to help you with a whole variety of things. So keep your eyes open for these events. These group programs can be very helpful. And once again, don't be like other students who say "I don't need it. I can figure it out on my own."

BE COLLEGE SMART. Always get good advice to keep in control of your life. It's really important. And always remember: You are the one who makes decisions for yourself. But to make good ones, you should listen to the advice and counsel of others. Speaking of which...

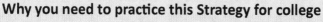

LISTEN TO DR. BOB —
Why you need to practice this Strategy for college

In college, you are first assigned a freshman adviser and later a major adviser. These are the people who help you plan and then approve your course schedule each semester, so you graduate on time.

Students who have good working relationships with their college advisers face fewer complications and frustrations.

However, advisers can do so much more. Want to talk about a possible major? Your adviser is the one to talk to. Think you might have to drop a course? You'd better get some advice first. Have a problem and don't know who to see about it? Start with your adviser. Working with any kind of adviser is a skill worth developing — one that you can use throughout your life.

And remember, good advice comes from all kinds of people in your life: for example, your parents, aunts and uncles, older brothers or sisters, your neighbors, and your parents' friends.

And don't forget your grandparents. Every time you see them, they ask you "How're things going? What're going to be when you grow up?" They have a lifetime of experience in certain areas that's absolutely invaluable. So make sure you take advantage of what all these people have to say. You'll get good advice from them, and they'll feel proud of you for asking.

 UP CLOSE AND PERSONAL

Elena doesn't understand her problem.

Elena did everything right to get ready for college. She took college-prep courses and worked hard to get the best grades. Early in her sophomore year, she started talking to her counselor and teachers about her college plans and interests. She selected six colleges she really liked, researched them on the Internet, and read about them in college reference books. A good talker, she visited each college and spoke with the right people to make sure she knew everything she could about the areas of study they offered, degree programs and requirements, dorm life, and financial aid.

She took time to prepare for the ACT and got great scores.

When her senior year started, Elena was ready to apply. She got strong letters of recommendation, and she was accepted by all six colleges, with very generous financial-aid packages. After some serious conversations with her counselor and parents, she made a good choice. She couldn't wait for the summer to end and for college to begin.

College began for Elena, but after one week, she knew something was wrong. **Because she was used to talking with teachers and counselors, she talked first with her Dorm Adviser, who referred her to me.**

In my first conversation with her, I couldn't believe anything could be wrong. Elena told me about her academic background and about her college plans. It was a pleasure to talk with such a completely friendly, well-spoken, and mature student.

When we got down to her problems, I told her to be simple and direct. Elena was. She said, "I don't like it here." I asked what, in particular, was wrong. Was it the dorm, her roommate, any of her courses? She said, "No, it's great here. It's everything I thought it would be. But," she went on, "I don't like being here. I don't know why. I'm uneasy all the time, and I'm sad being away from my family. I feel like at any minute I will just suddenly leave and go home."

Elena was homesick, very seriously homesick — to a degree I had not seen before. All college students experience some homesickness. For most students, the feeling lasts a few days or a couple weeks. However, once the loneliness and discomfort caused by being away from home are replaced by new friendships, new familiarities, and new comforts, the homesickness disappears.

I asked Elena to work with me, and I would help her get adjusted. I first phoned all of her professors and told them she needed a little encouragement. Then I invited Elena to come to my office each day and sit in my outer office to study. Part of her problem was that she needed a place "to belong." The office staff knew her, so the place was friendly and quiet, but no one bothered her. This temporary study place had helped other students feel rooted until they could move on to the library or a more traditional study place.

I encouraged her to make an appointment with the Counseling Center. And there were some other people I knew who were good at making students feel at home. I told her see them all, and she did.

After two weeks Elena saw me again and told me how grateful she was for all the help she received: "People have been so kind. I feel like they really care." "They do," I said. "We very much want students like you at our school." But I could see by the look in her eyes that her deepest feelings had not changed. So I asked, "If I were to give you a ticket home right now would you take it?" She said, *Without a second thought.* I said, "Okay, we did our best. Now it's time to do what you want, because this is your choice."

The next day, Elena and her mother were in my office to finalize her complete withdrawal from the college. I told them I was going to refund their tuition because Elena was experiencing a health problem, and they shouldn't be charged for something they couldn't anticipate.

Elena left my office feeling very grateful for the help of many people, very relieved that she was going home, very eager to deal with her problem with a psychologist, and very determined to start planning for a new college experience.

DEAN'S COMMENTARY

Elena represents many college students who, for any number of reasons, are not ready to start college.

At first glance, you might look at Elena's situation and feel sorry for her. But a second glance should make you understand that, under the circumstances, things could not have worked out better for her. The next time you really feel like you're in an impossible situation, think of Elena and start talking with people in the know — experts. You'll be surprised how even awful situations can be managed and solved with the right advice.

The importance of getting help. If Elena had not come for help, she would never have taken the initiative to withdraw from the university. Her grades would have gotten worse as the semester grew harder, and her frame of mind would have gotten worse with her grades. The college would have dropped her. She was in a can't-win situation.

Some problems are too large and too complicated for students to solve by themselves. That's why learning to talk to counselors and advisers is very important to your success as a student. Talking to an expert is the best way to go.

About being homesick. Homesickness can be a terrible adjustment problem for some students. Everything is new: roommates, cafeteria food, sleep patterns, and a class schedule unlike any the student has ever had. Family and close friends are absent, along with the comfortable feeling of home and neighborhood. Even though these students like campus, they miss their family and their home more. This is homesickness.

Going to college isn't like going to summer camp. It's not going to be over in a week or two. This is a commitment that seems to stretch out endlessly before the homesick student. For students with strong cases of homesickness, often the best solution is to admit that college away from home at this time of their lives is a mistake.

STRATEGY 7

Studying vs. homework —
*Did you know there's
a difference?*

* *

Learning something well is not that simple.
It takes energy, focus, and work. It's a
process that goes beyond doing homework
assignments. College Smart Students
complete their homework assignments
and then study the subject to master it.

LEARN ABOUT YOURSELF

Check all that apply.

How do you study?

☐ The night before a big test, I really hit the books.

☐ I want high grades, so I study as much as I can.

☐ I study "ahead" regularly, so I feel ready in each class.

☐ I don't have homework every night, so my study time varies.

☐ I study for every class almost every night.

☐ If a course is hard for me, I study harder for it.

☐ I usually don't work ahead. I find I work better under the stress of deadlines.

☐ I know that fish is brain food, so I eat a lot of fish sticks the day before a test.

☐ I put my book under my pillow each night and hope that I'll learn by osmosis.

☐ I believe that staying alert in class and taking a few notes is all I have to do.

IT'S A HUGE DIFFERENCE

Let's set the record straight with a couple simple definitions:

Homework:

- assignments given by a teacher, to be handed in and graded
- assignments teachers give to make sure students are keeping up

This homework keeps your mind focused as new material is presented in class. Homework helps you learn.

BE COLLEGE SMART.
But learning doesn't end with homework.
What else should you do?
Study.

Study:

Homework may help you stay on track, and that's good. **But the goal of study is long-term learning — learning that you take with you and use in college —** and that takes extra effort. This is more important than you can possibly know.

Studying has two goals:

- to get high grades
- AND keep that knowledge for a long time

For example, don't wait for teachers to tell you to re-read a chapter. Or rewrite your class notes. Or do extra "practice" problems, or spend more time studying if your grades are low. Doing all these things helps you learn your subject better.

Your job as a College Smart Student: to get as much knowledge out of the course as you can. And you want that knowledge to stick with you in your memory. And that happens only when you take the time to study in addition to doing the homework that your teacher assigns.

Crammers with great grades in high school will forget crammed info in a few days.

When they get to college and have to take an advanced course of a high school subject, they're already in trouble in the first week of class because they can't keep up. They don't remember enough to know what's going on in class.

If you're in college now, you have already come face to face with this particular lesson. If you're on your way to college, this is a HUGE point for you. Act on it right now.

STUDY = HIGH GRADES AND LONG-TERM LEARNING. CRUCIAL FOR COLLEGE

Repetition is crucial to your success

- **About notes.** Take class notes and then rewrite them later to give you another layer of learning. Re-writing your notes is another step in helping you remember all the details of the subject. Remember the cake?
- **Highlighting and outlining your textbooks.** Both are two more levels of learning. Highlight only on the second reading. That way, you have a better sense of what to highlight because you're familiar with the material this time around. On a first reading, you'll highlight too much.

Practice sharpens your learning skills.

Think of the learning you do each day in the same way you would prepare for an athletic event — working out, running and stretching exercises, ball handling, and so forth. To be the best in every game, athletes keep in shape and stay serious about what they're doing. It's a winning formula — a formula that every student should take to heart. Keep in mind that college is the NCAA of education.

Do what works best for you.

As you understand more about studying and how it works, you'll learn how to use repetition and organize course material to make learning more efficient and easier. Here's a list of studying methods that you could use to make you college smart. Practice them and learn them. **They're a formula for learning success in college.**

- Read ahead for the next class: Why? As the teacher presents new material, the class becomes a review for you. Smart, huh?
- Re-write (or re-key) to better organize class notes.
- Make outlines to see how the pieces fit together.
- Use flash cards.
- Make memory lists.
- Re-read chapters.
- Highlight important points.
- Review old tests to keep that material fresh in your mind.
- Complete extra practice problems.
- Diagram concepts.
- Draw pictures to help you remember concepts.
- Think about questions to ask in class.

Studying is very different from teacher-directed homework. Why? You have to take the initiative to do it. Studying and learning is a process. It takes time. Some students think that learning just happens. They think if they hear it in class, they've learned it. That's wrong-headed. As I've said before, learning comes in layers, and each layer makes learning stronger.

THE 4 BIG BENEFITS OF STUDY

1. **Excellent grades in all courses.** *A* students in college who are always *A* students know that high grades come not just from doing homework but from studying, too.
2. **What you learn sticks with you.** You'll still have it when you need it — years later in the workplace when you draw on knowledge you thought was totally unrelated to your career. You'll be surprised how much information you'll use and be glad you have it. Students who don't study regularly and cram at the last minute will draw a blank.

3. **Classes are another layer of studying and learning**. When you study in addition to doing homework, your classes will always make more sense to you, and you'll always learn more.

4. **Classes become exciting. You don't get bored in class.** You ask better questions, you participate more often, and you learn more. You're not just sitting in class, hoping to fill the hole in your head.

From now on, refer to all your schoolwork, in class and out, as studying, not homework. It will remind you of your true focus: succeeding in college. Homework is really something you do in grade school. And you're far beyond that.

I'LL SAY IT AGAIN. WHY? REPETITION LEADS TO LEARNING

- **Coming prepared for every class.** You're up to date in your reading, and you have even read ahead.
- **Reading ahead gives you an edge** and helps you learn your subject even better. To repeat: When your teacher introduces new material, it's reinforcing and adding to what you've already read.
- **Re-reading class material — and then taking notes and organizing** what you've read by making flashcards, outlines, lists, etc.
- **Taking good notes in class and then rewriting/organizing them as soon as possible — while the class is still fresh in your mind.** If you have a hard time keeping up with the teacher, record the class. (Ask the teacher if it's okay to do that.) Play back the class later and take notes at your own pace.
- **Reviewing graded tests and assignments.** You want to really understand why you got an answer wrong and figure out how to prevent that mistake on the next test.
- **Starting a writing assignment ahead of time.** That way, the paper can be roughed-out first and then re-written and improved before you hand it in.

- **Doing extra problems in math and science for practice.** It's a habit that makes sure you really understand certain concepts and formulas. It keeps your skills sharp.
- **Regularly reviewing <u>all</u> class notes every few weeks.** Otherwise, you're learning only the current chapter and forgetting the earlier ones as you plow ahead.
- **Asking the teacher questions after class if you've got questions.** Questions are good things. They signal that you're involved in the learning process.
- **The result?** You're always ready for the next big test. If you've been studying in all these ways, then, on the night before a test, **you won't have to CRAM.** And that means you're much more **relaxed and confident** when you take the test. It also means you'll remember the information when you need it later on.

 BE COLLEGE SMART. Keep in mind that all 12 Strategies lock together. They fit like puzzle pieces, and in the end, they show you the big picture of being a College Smart Student. If you use all of them you'll really make your life easier while you succeed.

DON'T MAKE EXCUSES FOR YOURSELF. YOU'RE TOO OLD FOR THAT!

- *"The teacher doesn't like me."* Teachers can't give high or low grades because they like or don't like you. Teachers are fair-minded. They give their students the grades they earn.
- *"The tests aren't fair."* Tests are only unfair if you haven't studied for them. True, some can be harder; some can be easier. The **College Smart Student** always studies as if *everything is going to be on every test.*

- *"The subject is too hard for me."* Subjects are supposed to get harder year after year. So each year, you have to increase your study time — especially on subjects that are more difficult for you.
- *"This course is useless."* How do you know what's useless? You can't see into the future. Life takes funny turns. Adults will tell you again and again that they've used many things that they never thought they would. That speech class will prepare you talk to people and groups in the workplace: and make a good impression.

WHICH COURSES ARE IMPORTANT?

Everything's important. True, you may find that some subjects are just more interesting to you than others. You won't love them all. But learning means achieving balance and becoming well-rounded, a broad thinker. That's how to become intelligent. I know you'd take advice from an Olympic medal winner in his or her sport. That's me. My sport is education. Believe me when I tell you this.

The College Smart Student studies math as much as English, science as much as history, and so forth. Finally, always remember that college requires that you take many of the same subjects that you took before. You can never leave a subject behind you just because you don't like it.

- You'll meet it again in college, and it will be harder and build on your high school coursework.

- Later in life, you'll find it would have been useful to know. You'll wish you'd learned it better. You just didn't foresee how you could use it. Life gives you surprises like that.

- Plus, you get an added benefit from every class you take. You learn to develop different thinking skills. Every class encourages you to expand your mind in different ways. And remember: the mind needs exercise, just like a muscle, to develop. The research proves it.

PLAGIARISM — not using your own brain and handing in someone else's work. That happens all the time. Using other people's work puts you in danger. It's also dishonest. Find out what you need to know in the FINAL NOTES section at the end of the book.

LISTEN TO DR. BOB —
Why you need to practice this Strategy for college

I've told you this before, and I'll say it again. College is a new experience. It's not high school away from home. It's different.

- College instructors pack twice the content in a semester.

- College semesters are shorter at the same time they're faster-paced.

- Tests are far fewer. Every test counts more. Low test grades turn into low final grades. There's rarely extra-credit to bring up low grades.

- Professors do not usually give homework to be handed in. It's up to you to follow the class outline and keep up.

- You have to study a lot! 25-30 hours for an average course load. It's like a full time job.

- A class often meets only 3 times a week. During class time, professors discuss a subject and tell you what to learn. Then, when you leave class, you're expected to spend time to learn independently, many more hours than in high school.

- Having all that unscheduled time outside of class means that you can choose when and if to study. So when you're not actually sitting in class, you have to control your time so you can study outside of class.

College students always have a lot of other things to do. Many are more fun than studying. But once you're in college, you have to balance fun and studying. You have to be responsible. You can still have fun and study. But don't forget that you have to give study top priority. And use your study time productively. Remind yourself that this education of yours is expensive. Get your money's worth.

In **Strategy 1,** we talked about using your brain as a processor. This Strategy tells you how to process information. In the next Strategy, I'll show you how to balance study with fun. It can be done, and you can do it!

College demands a lot, but it's also the key that opens doors to the rest of your life. So be college smart and use all my Strategies. The harder you work now, the more successful you'll be going forward and in your career.

 ## UP CLOSE AND PERSONAL

Marcus: A bright guy, but a slow learner

Marcus had always been a top student in high school and never had any problems. Now, in his fourth college semester, he was afraid he was going to lose his merit scholarship and his place in the honors program. His grades had been sliding since his freshman year. Marcus had come to see me this semester because although he had been an *A* student in high school, he had slid into the *B-* range in most of his college courses.

Marcus complained, "I'm doing the same thing now that I did in high school, when I got *A*s. I don't get it."

As I looked at Marcus's high school transcript, I saw that he had earned **only two *B*s** during his entire high school career, **one in Advanced Chemistry and one in an Advanced Placement American History course**. When I asked Marcus why he hadn't earned *A*s in those courses, too, he told me that the teachers had given really hard tests.

Marcus's ACT scores were in the 30s. That's high. Why couldn't he get *A*s in those two courses? Marcus didn't know. With his intelligence, this was an important question.

I asked Marcus how he prepared for tests. He told me that he went to class every day, listened carefully, did the homework, and studied hard the night before a test. He was a crammer — that had gotten him through high school with *A*s.

Correction: That *usually* earned him *A*s. Remember: He didn't earn *A*s in Advanced Chemistry and AP History. He couldn't get past a *B*. Why? Marcus was **a So-So Student.** He studied irregularly. *When he crammed, the good grades he received gave him the illusion that he was learning.* But he didn't study enough to earn *A*s in tough courses.

The *B*s were trying to tell him something, and being a **So-So Student,** he'd missed the point. When courses get harder, you must study harder to maintain *A* grades. And that's why he was in trouble now.

His college classes had gotten harder with every passing semester. He couldn't see that his old routine wasn't working — even though he'd had four semesters of low grades staring him in the face. He still clung stubbornly to his old routine, hoping that *next time* things would work out all right.

Quite simply, he wasn't doing enough. He needed to give his courses more energy and more time.

Since he couldn't evaluate his situation, I helped him. I introduced Marcus to the idea that studying for tests is actually an everyday process — from Day One of each semester and in every course. True, most tests still require some extra study time, a few days before the test to review to make sure that all the course material is still there at your fingertips.

As we talked, Marcus admitted that the only time he spent on courses outside of class was doing homework assignments. That's not anywhere near enough. In college, instructors expect you to study without assigning you work. Simply doing homework assignments will not put you in control of your courses.

Anybody can say a teacher gives hard or tricky tests, but if you know the material, that shouldn't matter. The fact is that Marcus got *B*s and *C*s because he didn't know how to study. He didn't know the material *well enough*. To save his scholarship, he had to really study and learn, not just treat college like high school.

⬆ DEAN'S COMMENTARY

At the beginning of our conversation, Marcus said to me, "I'm doing the same thing now that I did in high school, when I got *A*s. I don't get it."

I wanted to tell Marcus what students forget: College is harder than high school, so test-prep techniques that earned *A*s in high school might only earn *B*s (if that) in college. I didn't give him this answer because I thought there might be more to Marcus's story than that. There wasn't. It was simple. He just couldn't see it.

Marcus's solution was to study every day. That's the way to prepare for tests. You build a bank of knowledge a little at a time and add to it every day. Because you keep up with your work, you understand classroom presentations better, which makes the work you do outside of class easier and more meaningful.

Marcus had already proven that simply going to class, listening, doing assignments, and studying the night before the test didn't work anymore. His ACT scores told him he had the ability to succeed. However, if he didn't alter what he'd been doing, no dramatic change would take place.

Two changes had already taken place: He knew that he could no longer continue to say that his low grades were a mystery to him. Neither could he blame the teacher for being "hard." Professors are supposed to be harder: This is college.

If Marcus had continued to blame his professors for his falling grades, he would never have figured out how to succeed in school — or in life. When students say that tests are too hard, that's usually just an excuse. What's really going on? They still haven't accepted the fact that learning takes effort.

STRATEGY 8

Controlling Time
Creating a Personal Map—Fitting everything in your days (Finally!)

· ·

How often have you felt like you have so many things to do you can't possibly get them all done? There's no question that students are busy people — so busy that they often feel that there's not enough time in a day. They're stressed out and overwhelmed. What about you?

*Do you control your days, or
do they control you?*

*Do you find yourself robbing time from
one thing to make room for another?*

Do you let things go unfinished?

*Do you keep your fingers crossed
a lot before a test? Or pray!*

*Do you hope those pages you didn't have
time to study won't be on the test?*

*Do you hope you're "lucky"? That the
test will be easy? Or that the teacher
won't grade "hard" on your paper?*

*Do you find it difficult to fit homework
and study into your too-busy days?*

STRESSFUL, ISN'T IT?

If you answered yes to any of these questions, you need a **Personal Map.**
The idea is to map out your activities (including study) and stick to it. It's
how you organize your life. It's what you'll have to do in the workplace and
family life. It's known as being able to juggle multiple priorities.

Creating a **Personal Map** is one of the most important things you can
do for yourself. It will not only get you ahead of the game, but as you move
ahead in school, you'll always be able to control harder challenges. It will
be a real advantage to you in the workplace, too.

LEARN ABOUT YOURSELF

Remember how you mapped out time for all of your activities in **Who are you, deep down inside?** Go back and look at it now. If you were honest in listing what fills your day, do you see how packed your days are? How much time did you label as school work OUTSIDE of your school day?

When you worked out that **Weekly Activity Map,** you didn't understand as much about being a **College Smart Student** as you do now. Now you have a better idea of how you should use your time. You now understand your many roles and responsibilities — what you have to do. You also now realize that some activities are more important than others. Studying is more important than texting. Learning is more important than napping. School is more important than vegging-out.

MAPPING OUT TIME REALLY HELPS!

The thought of making a Map, much less sticking to it, makes a lot of students cringe. They say:

- *"Who needs it?"*
- *"I always know what I have to do."*
- *"When I **have** to do things at certain times, it cramps my style."*

But the truth is that following a Map doesn't cramp your style. A Map makes your life a lot easier, even if the idea doesn't sound like it.

- You'll feel a great sense of accomplishment.
- You'll reduce the stress in your life.
- You'll get everything done that you need to.
- You'll be in control of your entire life.
- And you'll feel great!

THE 3 STEPS TO PERSONAL MAP MAKING

Here we go! Time for you to make your own **Personal Map**. I'll guide you along the way.

	Sun	Mon	Tue	Wed	Thu	Fri	Sat
7:00							
8:00							
9:00							
10:00							
11:00							
12:00							
1:00							
2:00							
3:00							
4:00							
5:00							
6:00							
7:00							
8:00							
9:00							
10:00							
11:00	Go to Bed!	Go to Bed!	Go to Bed!	Go to Bed!	Go to Bed!		
Total							

Step 1 — How many hours do you need?

Fact: As a college freshman, you should be studying 25-30 hours each week. And that increases with each year.

Whether you're in middle school, high school or college already, developing **a Personal Map** is crucial. What I'm telling you in Step 1 is that —

- If you're in middle school, you have to get ready for high school.
- If you're in high school, you have to look ahead to college.
- If you're in college, you have to start right now!

Whatever level of school you're in, you always have to increase your study hours as you enter a new school year.

The chart below shows what a high school student should do. A middle schooler might study fewer hours than a high schooler. However, in college, you have to study more — a lot more.

Given your year in school, are you anywhere near these numbers?

Year of High School	Minimum Number of Study Hours Each Week
Freshman Year	5 hours
Sophomore Year	10 hours
Junior Year	15 hours
Senior Year	20 hours
Year in College	**Minimum Number of Study Hours Each Week**
Freshman Year	25-30 hours

If you're still in high school, you now have a guide. This is how you work your way up to freshman year in college: studying **25-30 hours each week**. If you're already in college, you'll need to get up to this study time as so soon as you can. You'll find these freshman hours will probably increase as you move up the ranks in college.

Again, it's like an athlete: Competing in college requires a lot more practice time and effort than high school.

So if you've been paying attention, you realize that this Strategy acts as the structure, the backbone, of the other 11 Strategies. It gets you through your days so you can use the other Strategies. Now that you understand the importance of learning, you know that learning is "your job." Let's figure out what you need to do now to get in shape to handle those hours.

Step 2 — Learn as you go

After you see how you're doing early in the semester, you'll know how your study effort is paying off. You'll know whether or not your study hours are okay or if they need to be bumped up.

Even during the semester, you may have to move your hours up to get prepared for a big assignment. Then you can return to your normal routine. Your **Map** flexes as needed.

See how you can control things? And when you're in control, your stress goes down, and you'll feel great!

Step 3 — Putting it all together

In making a **Personal Map,** let's divide the things in your life into 4 different categories:

1. What you do for **Personal Enjoyment**, like being with your friends, playing sports or computer games, spending time online and texting
2. Extracurricular **Activities**, lessons, practices, clubs, *etc.*
3. Responsibilities to your **Family or Job**, helping out at home
4. And the big thing: **Studying**

If you're in middle school or high school, you study mostly in the

evening. **If you're in college, you study when you have open time in your day or evening.**

How much <u>can</u> be done? When you use your list to start filling in your **Personal Map,** you'll find that maybe you're trying to do too much every day. It may be impossible to fit it all in and that's why you feel stressed all the time. This is a hard lesson, but it's a life lesson everyone faces. None of us can do everything we'd like to do in a single day. There's only so much time.

Ranking things. True, most things you do in life are important to you. But some you can live without doing every day. Which things can you drop on a busy day when you have other commitments that can't be moved or dropped? Maybe you have to move your music lesson to a day when you don't have an extracurricular meeting. You're taking control of your days, and you'll feel better because of it. But it might take some getting used to.

Trading time. It's a sign of maturity that you understand you can't have it all every day. Perhaps things trade off. Perhaps some things you do Mondays and Thursdays; you do other things on Tuesdays and Wednesdays. When you were a child, you didn't like to be denied. But now juggling priorities is a part of life and you're old enough to understand that.

Making important choices. Studying always has to be your top priority. If your volleyball coach suddenly decides you have to practice three hours a day, you have a decision to make. (My son's coach did this.) You have study *and many other things* that you'd like to do. Releasing volleyball suddenly opens up your day. Or keep volleyball and study but release your other activities: phone time, text time, *etc.*

- Study must always fit into your list of things to do.
- And if you study by following your **Personal Map,** you'll see how much time you have to play with.
- You'll learn to organize your days to fit more things that you want to do into your life.
- The big lesson: Time is finite. You can't think without sleep. Not being realistic about time stresses your days.

COLLEGE GIVES YOU LOTS OF FLEX TIME. MAP IT OR LOSE IT.

The real need to control your time. With fewer classes scheduled in a week, and more independent time, you need more control to use time the way you want to. You don't want it just to disappear on you. That happens really easily. So you rely on your **Personal Map** to take care of you.

But because you have more unstructured time, you have to keep track of it — recording things like "Coffee at the Union with Mark, 10:00, Community Outreach Meeting, 4:30, Band practice, 6:00, and so forth.

WARNING: Don't make the mistake of plugging in study time very late in the day when you're too tired to think. No matter where you are in school, you need a sharp mind to study.

After you've created your Personal Map —

1. **E-mail it to others.** Then they'll know to respect the time when you're studying and need to be alone. Remember Kirsten in **Strategy 2?** She made sure her friends had copies of her **Map.**

2. **Use it to react to change.** If your chem teacher tells the class that an upcoming chapter is really difficult, take out your **Map** and figure out how to find a bit more time for that subject that week.

3. **You're in control.** You can see what you're doing. Because you can see all the things you do right there on your **Map,** you can work with them!

Outside of study time, you have two groups of personal activities: 1) unscheduled, social/relaxation activities and 2) athletics, part-time job, music lessons, and so forth. This second group must be mapped into your days. They get a higher priority than #1 group.

SOME TIPS ON MAPPING

Keep these details in mind when you fill out your **Personal Map.**

- Be patient. Filling out a **Personal Map** takes time
- Make your **Personal Map** simple and easy for anybody to follow.
- Your mind likes routine, so routine helps you study better. Stick to your map.
- Don't ignore or disregard your easier courses.
- Give all subjects the time they deserve. If a certain class is harder for you, add extra time.
- Big tests and assignments coming due? Add time to your regular study time if you need to.
- Study regularly. It eliminates the need to cram.
- If you have to drop some study hours for whatever reason (an unexpected appointment), be sure *you make them up.*
- Take study breaks. Get a snack, get something to drink, and then come back to your studying. Don't take a break and get involved in something like texting or a TV show that will pull you away from your studying for too long a time.
- To be a good studier, you need to eat, sleep, and exercise each day. Ignoring your health is bad news.

Sticking to your Personal Map will give you a feeling of great accomplishment every day — day after day. You've got it all together!

MAPS PREVENT HITTING THE GLASS WALL

What is a glass wall? Here're a couple of examples:

- A student takes a test and wham! He gets a low grade. He's just run into a glass wall.
- A student turns in a paper and POW! She gets a low grade. It's another glass wall.

Glass walls are what students run into when they don't follow a **Map.** They take tests they aren't prepared for. They turn in assignments that they didn't take enough time for. They don't know that they've done this until it's too late. That's why it's a glass wall. They don't see it until they hit it.

When they get low grades, they say, "Well it's not my fault. The test was too hard." Or "I didn't have enough time for that assignment." They're kidding themselves.

When you follow a well-planned **Map,** you'll always be ready for that next test and that next assignment. No glass walls for you.

There are so many things involved in getting good grades —

- the challenges of the class
- the demands of the teacher
- the kinds of tests and assignments given
- how good you are in a subject
- how many other things you have going on in your life
- how committed you are to doing well in everything

So many variables. And you've got to control them.

When I talk about controlling your life and your classes, I'm talking about following a **Personal Map.** Yes, you can have a great study place, and you can understand what it means to study, but if you can't make the time in your day to study, nothing happens.

Starting now, take control of your days. You are the only one who can. **It's called time management.** Think of it this way:

Your Map —

1. **Separates study time from everything else in your life.** This separation reminds you that you need to study every day. It gets the job done!

2. **Prevents the less important things in your life from taking over** — from getting between you and studying, between you and managing your time. All are skills you need to be a **College Smart Student.**

3. **Lets you be flexible**. It enables you to increase the amount of time when you need to in a subject. Also, when something comes up, you just adjust your days to protect the number of study hours. It's easy to figure out how to do it. Everything's there on your **Map**. It helps you make good choices.

4. **Takes pressure and anxiety out of your life.** It keeps you clear-headed, and that's really important.

ABOUT PART-TIME JOBS

They're good in a lot of ways...

1. You earn extra money.
2. You learn how to follow a schedule.
3. You learn how to be responsible in a workplace.
4. You learn how to work well with others.
5. You learn how to follow directions carefully.

...But with a part-time job you have to be careful.

- You can't work too many hours each week. Don't turn a part-time job into a half-time job. Your employer may push you to do that.
- You may want to work more to earn extra money. But you have to get in those study hours, your extracurricular hours, and your important personal hours.
- Too many work hours make that impossible. You don't want work hours to cut into the equally important things in your life, especially studying.

How to handle jobs
- **During the semester,** work no more than 10-15 hours a week, and try to work those hours on the weekends if you can.
- **During the summer,** it's really good to work a full time job — for all the same reasons as working a part-time job. Earn your money in the summer, so you don't have to work during school time. Select a good job that involves a lot of responsibility.

BE COLLEGE SMART. Make studies your first priority. Working a job is good experience. But unless that job is your goal in life, study comes first.

Discover the dangers in how students use free time. Go to the FINAL NOTES section at the end of the book.

Some college students spend great amounts of their out-of-class time in ways that are really dangerous — both psychologically and academically. And as students, they always fail.

Get started on your Personal Map right now. It may be a little hard at first. You may have to change it a little bit here and there and move things around before you get the hang of it. But when you have it in your hands, it'll feel good right away. You'll say to yourself, "This is my personal map. I made it. When I follow it, I'm in charge." This is a huge step for you in getting control.

LISTEN TO DR. BOB —
Why you need to practice this Strategy for college

Mapping means organizing your life. When your life is organized, you enjoy everything more, and you feel great about yourself because you're in control.

Remember we compared your education to climbing a mountain? As you move up the mountain (education), everything gets more difficult. But when you're in control of your life and everything you have to do, what seems to be really difficult becomes, instead, challenging, exciting, and fulfilling. When you get to the top, you'll raise your hands and say, "YESSSS!! I made it!"

Keep a positive outlook, set your goals clearly, work hard, and you'll reach that summit and see a view of the wonderful career and life ahead of you.

UP CLOSE AND PERSONAL

Carol Ann: You see, my canary ...

Carol Ann had charm! Meet her once and you'll feel like a friend. On campus, everyone knew her. Put her in a classroom, however, and the professor, when handing back tests, ignores her sweet smile and just glares.

I had met her once before, and her charm distracted me so much I accepted her comment, *"Oh, I'm doing fine. No problemo!"*

One year later, she had *problemos*. She came in to see me.

Carol Ann: Dr. Bob, you are looking great. Even younger than ...

Dr. Bob: (I interrupted.) How are you doing?

Carol Ann: Oh, I think ....

(I cut her off again.)

Dr. Bob: I don't believe you're *thinking* at all! I said it with emphasis.

Carol Ann: You're sounding like my dad.

Dr. Bob: But I'm not paying your tuition. If I were, people would hear me yelling at you across campus. After three semesters, your GPA is 2.2, and you've completed only 35 credits when you should be at 45.

Carol Ann: (pauses before speaking.)

Carol Ann: My canary has been sick.

Dr. Bob: I stared at her for at least 30 seconds. I leaned back in my chair, saying, "Oh, I have to hear this."

Carol Ann: At the beginning of the year I was really ready to go. But then my canary developed this cough.

Another 30 seconds passed.

Dr. Bob: (A cough...)

Carol Ann: You know, instead of tweeting, (Carol Ann tweeted), he sort of coughed (Carol Ann coughed). So I took him to the vet. It was hard to get an appointment. Lots of sick birds out there. (LOL)

Dr Bob: (I leaned forward on my desk and held my head in both hands.)

Carol Ann: The vet said my canary was suffering from second-hand smoke. You know I smoke.

Dr. Bob: Yes, Carol Ann. I smelled you coming through the door.

Carol Ann: Basically, it comes down to this. I love my canary, so now I have to smoke outside. That means I have to go down four flights of stairs to get outside and then I ...

Dr. Bob: I get the picture. (I gave her one of my stare-into-your-soul looks.) Except for smoking, I think you're an intelligent person. So, instead of my telling you, you tell me what you should be doing, including going to a smoking cessation class.

Carol Ann: This is like a pop quiz.

Dr. Bob: ...And your college career depends on it.

Carol Ann: Okay, I can do this. Just let me think. You see, I can think if I have to.

She spent a minute moving around in her chair.

Carol Ann:

> *Number 1:* I should study in a routine.
>
> *Number 2:* I should go to class more often.
>
> *Number 3:* I should study more for tests.

How am I doing?"

Dr. Bob: No answer.

Carol Ann: Number, what number am I on? Oh yes, 4. I should see someone. Maybe I have a learning disability. What do you think? Did I pass?

Dr. Bob: Carol Ann, your only disability is that you don't know how to be a college student.

Carol Ann: That's rather blunt, but I take your point. So what do I do?

Dr. Bob: You have to figure that out. Good grief, you've been in college for over three semesters. Make two lists:

> *List 1:* What are you doing wrong?
>
> *List 2:* What do you have to do to make things right?

Carol Ann: Is this another test?

Dr. Bob: Do you have the answers?

Carol Ann left my office, moving her head up and down and already using her fingers to count off items or points. I knew she was already making her lists.

⤴ DEAN'S COMMENTARY

I could have used stories about the students who lost their dreams because they couldn't handle their time. I chose not to. Carol Ann is a real story (not her real name.) I wanted to make the point without a tragic ending.

Carol Ann turned her failures into successes. She learned the important lesson that getting on the right track most often means looking carefully at the wrong track.

She knew she had to study more. She honestly admitted she was a minimal, last minute studier.

If she wanted to study more, she had to keep track of her study hours. At college orientation, her adviser said college was a full time job — so study 30-40 hours each week. (She recalled saying to herself, *"Yeah, right!"*) She had been a completely casual student doing what she wanted and when. That needed to change. So she set up a **Weekly Map** with study as her top priority.

In the end, and after a few more discussions with me, Carol Ann figured out all the things she was doing wrong. She even figured out what she had to do to fix them. As I started writing my book, I often thought of Carol Ann. She and many other students like her, inspired me to help you. She took my advice and became successful. She graduated on time with a high GPA— despite three semesters of low grades. A very hard thing to do.

And guess what she's doing now? She works in public relations for one of the largest school systems in the country. She learned how to put her charm, her knowledge, and her intelligence into one effective package.

You could use a computer calendar to build your **Map**, or if you prefer, a pencil-and-eraser method, here's a "working copy" to just rough things in. You can always go to www.GetCollegeSmart to print more copies to use to develop different versions for this semester.

	Sun	Mon	Tue	Wed	Thu	Fri	Sat
7:00							
8:00							
9:00							
10:00							
11:00							
12:00							
1:00							
2:00							
3:00							
4:00							
5:00							
6:00							
7:00							
8:00							
9:00							
10:00							
11:00	Go to Bed!	Go to Bed!	Go to Bed!	Go to Bed!	Go to Bed!		
Total							

STRATEGY 9

All about tests—
*a way for you to
measure progress*

· ·

In one way or another, your life will be filled with tests, even after you've finished school. So you need to become a good test-taker. When you have a job, and your boss says, "I'd like you to solve this problem." That's a "test." Are you thinking of buying a new car? You *have to answer the question, "Can I afford it?" That's a test, too. So let's look at the tests you take in school, and see if, together, we can make you a better test-taker.*

 ## LEARN ABOUT YOURSELF

On a scale of 1 (lowest) to 5 (highest), rate yourself on these test-preparation strategies.

- ☐ Preparing for tests without cramming.

- ☐ Reviewing graded tests to see what you got wrong and why.

- ☐ Keeping a file of the tests you've taken for each class.

- ☐ Guessing what questions will be on the next test.

- ☐ Getting advice when you've gotten a low grade.

- ☐ Studying more for your next test when you've just gotten a low test grade.

- ☐ Talking to your teacher before hard tests.

- ☐ Recording test dates on your calendar so they can never sneak up on you.

Imagine going into a test. You're nervous; you're worried; maybe you're sweating a little bit. Before you sit down, if someone asks you, *"Hey, what's up, dude?"* What would your answer be?

Let's imagine you're going into another test. You're confident; you're relaxed. You're really up for it. And you want to show-off what you know. So, what's the difference? It all has to do with preparation.

TAKE A TEST. GO PLACES.

Why are you a student? Well, to learn — and to learn *how to learn*. But very practically, you're in school because you eventually want to have a great career. The path to any career is filled with tests.

Many students don't see the connection between —

(a) what they do in school each day, like taking tests, and
(b) what they will have to do on a job.

Here's the connection. No matter what your future career or job, you will be tested every day by other people. That's what a job is. You get that job because you have the knowledge and skills to answer questions and solve problems. Sounds a lot like a test, doesn't it? It is!

Tests are a fact of life, part of every career. In fact, you have to pass tests just to get to a career. You may as well start learning now how to deal with tests if you want to succeed in life.

YOU'RE IN FOR A FUTURE OF ANSWERING QUESTIONS

One of the main purposes of being in school is to make you a good problem solver or test-taker. When you take a test, you're —

- gaining knowledge,
- developing learning skills,
- becoming a better thinker.

Put it another way: By taking tests, you're using your knowledge and thinking skills. It's a talent you'll use later on in life.

Think about this. When you get a low grade on a test, you can bring it up on the next one. Getting a low grade on a job is much more serious. You may not get a second chance.

- If you're an automotive engineer, making a mistake could lead to thousands of accidents.

- If you're a stockbroker who makes a bad decision, your clients can lose thousands of dollars.
- If you're a doctor and you make a mistake, someone could die.

So later on in life, when someone on the job asks you, *"What do I do now?"* You'll have the right answer. Or if you ask yourself, *"How do I solve this problem?"* You'll know how to do it. Why? Because in school, you learned how to be a good test-taker.

In life, there's no un-do key.

MORE YOU CAN LEARN FROM ATHLETES AND MUSICIANS

If you ask athletes what they like the most about a sport, the answer would be *PLAYING IT.* Practicing for the game is okay because it's necessary. They need to do things, like exercises, wind sprints, or weight-lifting. But when they're out on the field using their skills, their blood really gets going. To win the game, the challenge is to use what they practiced.

Ask musicians why they enjoy what they do, and their answer would probably be like the athletes'. They would say, "I know that I have to practice. And I couldn't play my instrument if I didn't." But it's performing and hearing the audience's cheers and applause along with the pride I take in my progress that makes all the practice worthwhile."

So why is it that when you're a student, you don't like tests? Aren't they just like winning the game or putting on a great show? Don't you want your teacher (coach) to be proud of you? Don't you want your parents to feel the same way? So what you have to do is look at tests in school in a different way.

Look at them just like the athlete and the musician. Studying is like practice. You have to do it. Then whenever you take a test, think of it as a way to show how good you are — how well you've practiced. The test is the big game or the big performance.

ABOUT TAKING TESTS: BEFORE, DURING, AND AFTER

You've probably read lots of tips about preparing for and taking tests. You know, getting enough sleep, reading questions carefully, checking your answers, etc. The tips are good. Here're some more ideas about tests. Some may be familiar — some may be new to you. All are important.

Before the test

Talk to your teacher if you're unsure about some of the class material. Do this several days before the test. Don't wait until the last minute. Just hoping that the material you don't "get" won't be on the test is about as good as crossing your fingers and hoping for the best.

Study everything, even though you know that everything can't be on the test. No test covers everything you had in the class. But you should study everything anyway. Knowing as much as you can is essential to developing test-taking skills.

Practice, practice, practice. Just as you practice free throws for basketball or learn your lines for a play, you prepare for tests every day. How do you do that? Let me remind you:

- Listening carefully in class
- Learning as you go
- Keeping up with and staying slightly ahead of your class
- Doing homework carefully
- Studying with concentration

You want to develop a routine:

- Do extra science problems
- Re-read and re-organize your class notes
- Re-read the chapter
- Outline important information
- Create charts and flash cards

Review your Study Brief. What's a Study Brief? It's all the key information that you've studied for class written out on one or two sheets of paper. Your Study Brief helps you view those key highlights of your class at a glance. It's like getting pumped up before getting onto the field or the court.

Just *making* a Study Brief is a form of studying. As you wait for the test to be passed out, give your Study Brief one more look. Then your mind is ready to go.

Don't procrastinate. Has this ever happened to you? You've got a few days before a test and a little voice in the back of your head starts saying, "I know that I'm not ready to take Thursday's test, but I think I know enough. I'll risk it. I can hold off and just study Wednesday night. It'll be okay."

- This is typical procrastinator talk. Students who put off daily study already suspect they have big holes in their knowledge. For them, studying a few days before the test is really scary. It tells them just how much they ***don't*** know.
- It would be a lot of work to catch up. They don't want to face it. So they choose to wait until the last minute to cram and hope for the best.

Don't cram. Most students review seriously right before any test, especially big tests — that's natural. But there's a big difference between *a reviewer* and *a crammer.*

For crammers, this last minute preparation is the only prep they have done for the test. If there weren't tests, these students probably wouldn't study at all. They'd skim the surface of their courses from day to day. They'd hardly learn anything.

One of the main reasons that you have tests in school is to keep you motivated and on-track. But it doesn't work for crammers. Crammers wait until the night before the test. Then they really plunge into course material to cram, running at full speed. They may even pull an all-nighter.

The crammer hopes the information will stay in his or her brain just long enough to get through the test. Some students get really good at cramming — they even get pretty good grades on tests they've crammed for.

The real danger of cramming is this: The knowledge gained is temporary.

It's called short-term learning, and it means your mind hangs onto information for only a brief time. Then, after the test, **the information disappears for good because crammers never really learned it in the first place.**

Crammers finish courses, semesters, and even years of school with little or no knowledge. When they get to college, they've long-forgotten what they should have learned before.

These students don't have the knowledge to keep up with college courses. Cramming is one of the major reasons that huge numbers of students drop courses, drop out of college or take extra years to finish a degree. Cramming means needing LOTS more money for college.

But that won't happen to you. You're not a crammer. You're a **College Smart Student.**

During the test

Here are some basic tactics to help you make the best use of your test-taking time.

Read test questions CAREFULLY. It's the #1 rule when taking any test. In fact, read every question at least twice before you answer it. There is nothing worse than getting a test back and seeing that you lost points on a question when you knew the right answer! You just misunderstood what the question was asking.

Always read the test from beginning to end before you answer any questions. Some students are afraid to discover the hard questions that come later in the test. To do your best, you have to know what you're dealing with from the start.

Most of the time, you don't have to answer questions in any particular order. Use this freedom to your advantage. You can answer the questions in any order that is comfortable for you. Do the easy questions first (to score sure points right away) or the hard ones first (to get them off your mind). Do what works best for you.

Gather your thoughts. Close your eyes for a few seconds before you start the test. Use this time to relax your mind and relax your breathing.

Wear a watch or sit where you can see a clock. Don't lose track of time. If you do, you likely won't get to all the questions.

Skim each section of the test. Estimate how long each section will take to complete. Now keep an eye on the clock, so you can pace yourself and complete all the test questions.

Don't understand a question? Raise your hand and ask the teacher, "Do you mean ...?"

Handling essay/paragraph answers. Jot down key points before starting to write. Follow them carefully. Don't run the risk of forgetting one of those points or rambling off the main points and never returning to them.

Don't leave any essay question blank. Even if you're struggling with the question, write whatever you know that relates to the question. You might get some points.

Take care of personal needs. Make sure you go to the bathroom before a test. Dress comfortably. Get tissues or cough drops if you have a cold.

Crunched for time? Work on the questions with higher point values.

Check for careless mistakes. If time permits, go over your answers to catch errors caused by stress.

Stay focused. Don't let small annoyances distract you: the siren on the street outside, the kid who taps his pencil or blows his nose. If the door down the hall bangs, don't look up. None of it is important at the moment. Ignore it all and concentrate on the test.

When you get the test back

Wrong answers are just as important as right answers. When you get a test back, don't just look at the grade and then throw the test in your backpack or in the trash can. Look at those wrong answers. Ask yourself, "Did I get them wrong because I didn't know the answer, or because I made a careless error?"

- If your grade is the result of not knowing the subject well enough, there are two obvious remedies.

◊ Put in more time studying

◊ See your teacher (or your guidance counselor) about your study habits. Maybe you need to change your **Personal Map**. Perhaps you're missing a better or smarter way to tackle this subject.

- If you have a pattern of careless errors, recognize it, and be more careful next time.

  ◊ Getting enough sleep?

  ◊ Not reading directions carefully?

  ◊ Not looking at the entire test before you start so you can pace yourself?

If you don't understand why you got an answer wrong, go over your test with the teacher. And don't go to the teacher just to argue for extra points. You need to figure out what you misunderstood, so you don't make the same mistakes on the next test.

When your test grade is low

You may not want to admit it, but test grades are your fault. Not the fault of the teacher. Not the fault of the subject, which you might not like. And not the fault of the tests you're taking. The worst thing a test-taker can do is make excuses or assign blame to others.

You must learn to take tests effectively and accurately. Poor test-takers don't understand that test-taking is a skill. It must be developed from test to test and year to year to get really ready for a career. Read on.

THE BIG-TIME: STANDARDIZED TESTS

PSATs, ACTs, SATs, LSATs, MCATs —There's a whole alphabet of 'em! College admissions tests — SATs ACTs, and APs — are your first experience with qualifying tests. Your scores on these tests either open or close doors to college. You need to take the time to prepare seriously for them. Here's the good news: By spending time preparing for them carefully, you will get high scores.

As much as you've developed test-taking skills in your courses, you'll need to develop some new test-taking skills just for standardized tests. Visit the SAT and ACT web sites. They give very good introductions to these tests. Log on and learn about them. Also get some prep books or software or log-on to Internet sites that help you practice. Use these tools. Practice is proven to boost your score.

Standardized tests are just part of your life as long as you're in school. The thing to remember is that they require a lot of preparation so you get a high score the first time you take them. If you score low because you didn't prepare, you'll need to take the test again. Develop your skills for taking standardized tests NOW so they don't become an obstacle to entering college, or graduate school (like medical or law school) or a career later on.

LISTEN TO DR. BOB —
Why you need to practice this Strategy for college

Become a skillful test-taker now so that you're a better one in college. There, tests are harder because classes are harder. Unlike high school teachers, who may give dozens of quizzes and tests in a semester, college instructors may give only a midterm and a final exam. When you have only two or three tests per course, your grade on each one is critical. And each of those grades determines your final grade.

Some students like to wait to see what they get on the first test before they decide how much they have to study for a course. That's just not smart. You can't afford to take that risk. In college, if you mess up on the first test out of three, you're in trouble.

Here's another reason that test performance is critical. Your test grades in college can't be improved by that old high school remedy: doing extra-credit. Some high school students have gotten into the habit of asking for extra-credit projects to offset not-so-good test grades. Don't get into that habit. Extra-credit hardly ever exists in college — test grades stand on their own.

Whenever you feel down and wonder why you have to spend time learning, recall that your life after graduation requires the same skills you need in school. So even if you don't always like the daily school routine, **maintain your respect for it**. Because when the curtain goes up on the opening night of your life after college graduation, you want to know your part really well — well enough to get the applause you deserve in the form of success and rewards.

Look at your answers in this Strategy's LEARN ABOUT YOURSELF. The items are really a list of ways to prepare for tests. How does your approach to tests right now stack up to tips in the list? How much of this info did you already know?

Congratulate yourself on everything you're doing right!

Go back through the Strategy and put a check mark in the margin next to each point you have to work on. As the school year progresses, return to your checked sections frequently to see how you're improving.

 ## UP CLOSE AND PERSONAL

Jason: Your Basic So-So Student

In high school, Jason bragged that he always got high grades in all his classes. But the truth was that he got only *some* high grades in *some* of his classes. Nevertheless, he was proud as a peacock of what he thought of as his unique accomplishments. And he showed his proud, bright feathers to everyone: his teachers and counselors in particular. They would reply without enthusiasm, "Yes, Jason very good." Jason thought that he was great!

Although Jason got some high grades, he earned his highest grades in two subjects: Cramming and Procrastination. Let me define them with regard to learning.

- **Procrastination** means waiting until the last possible minute to write a paper or to study for a test.
- **Cramming** is what procrastinators do the night before a test and the night before a paper is due.

Jason, more than anyone, knew these terms. He was an expert at both. In his sleep, Jason dreamed of a double major in college: (You guessed it.) **Cramming and Procrastination.** He knew he would succeed. He usually did. In fact, he could have taught college courses in both subjects:

In Cramming 101, students would be graded on the shortness of time between studying and taking every test.

- If they studied the night before a test, they would get a *C* in Jason's course.
- If they studied while walking to the class to take the test, they got a *B*.
- Best of all, if they studied while the professor handed out the test, they got an *A*.

In Procrastination 102, students would be graded on how long it took them to turn in an assignment after it was due.

Granted, this is a silly story about Jason. But, unfortunately, there are a lot of Jasons out there. They have no clue about –

- Organizing their life
- Making school a priority in their life
- Taking learning seriously

- Setting goals for the future
- Studying as a learning process
- The value of knowledge, or
- Becoming a mature individual – independent and purposeful

Put all of these deficiencies together, and we have a student who not only accomplishes little or nothing in school, but actually interferes with what teachers and more dynamic students are trying to do each day: both in and out of the classroom. For example, Jason never contributes to class discussion. He and students like him just sit there like rude people. Put several "Jasons" in a class, and both teachers and students actually feel and react to this disinterest. Teachers have to tolerate them. Students try to pretend the Jasons aren't there.

Also, because Jason believes he really is an accomplished student, he mocks other students for being serious. "You mean you really study that much? I'm a fast learner. I don't have to study." Or, when he does get a low grade on a test, his reaction is always "That teacher doesn't like me," or "I didn't know that was going to be on the test."

If a couple students talk to the teacher after class, there is Jason trying to push his way into the group. The teacher just knows that Jason will be —

- Complaining about his grade on the last test
- Making an excuse for not doing well. (He's been so overworked lately that he couldn't concentrate.)
- Asking to take the test over — he just knows he can do better
- Asking to turn in a late paper because he lost his lap top or the dog ate it
- Begging to do extra-credit work to make up for all his low grade(s)

Jason, to give him some credit, could actually be a nice guy. With his friends, he wasn't out to be disagreeable or rude. He just wanted to beat the system.

And from long experience as a procrastinator and crammer, Jason knew that flattering with great courtesy was a skill to develop with teachers and people of authority.

As Jason moved from year to year in school, and eventually to college, his excuses became more ridiculous, his begging became intolerable, and his presence was avoided by teachers and students alike.

Here's another big change. He hit a wall in college. His flattering and excuses that were beginning to fail him in his later years of high school **didn't work at all in college.**

When his tried and true personal strategies completely failed, he still didn't understand what went wrong. But one thing he was sure of: It wasn't his fault! Then, after he was asked to leave college because of his poor grades, he decided college wasn't that important. He consoled himself with the thought that Bill Gates never finished at Harvard.

But unlike Mr. Gates and his genius, Jason continued to fail as an employee, even in menial jobs. Even his family didn't want to listen to him complain anymore. Life was so cruel!

"Well," he said to himself, "I'm sure things will turn out better sooner or later. Something will come my way. I just have to be patient."

⟲ DEAN'S COMMENTARY

The lessons to be learned from Jason are very obvious. When you look at the list of things Jason never learned as a student, it's easy to see why he failed as a person — even to the point of sitting around waiting for an opportunity to knock on his door. As Jason grows older, his life doesn't fulfill his expectations.

As I've said before, school and learning get harder from one year to the next. That's what school is all about. You may stumble now and then, but you always pick yourself up and find your footing again. That's what you will have to do in life whether we're talking about developing a career or a personal life of accomplishment and satisfaction.

Think of it this way: You know I've said many times that learning HOW to learn is as important as WHAT you learn. That's a really big point, but it's not the only thing you should learn as a student. If you grow and mature as a student, you'll grow and mature as a person. Grow as a person, and life will always be a welcome challenge that gives you great satisfaction and accomplishment.

Admire and imitate those students who *have-it-all-together*. Join their club. Become president of that club, and you'll be a role model for students around you. Ultimately, you'll have control of your life, and the feeling will be great.

STRATEGY 10

Tracking grades—*getting from here to there takes more than hope and luck*

. . . .

As you move through a semester, do you ever pause to figure out how well you're doing in each of your classes? Or do you just "wait and see" what your final grade will be?

That's a little like whitewater kayaking without a paddle: You're letting the

123

rapids sweep you along. You should be controlling the kayak so that you don't hit the rocks or capsize! This Strategy will give you the paddle to steer yourself safely through each semester's waters.

LEARN ABOUT YOURSELF

Check all the statements that describe you.

How do you think about the grades that you get during the semester?

☐ I don't think about grades. I just take each test and assignment as it comes. Whatever they add up to will be my final grade.

☐ I have a vague idea of my grades because I try to remember them. Sometimes grades on report cards surprise me because I thought I was doing better than I actually was.

☐ I worry about grades a lot. So I really hope for the best.

☐ I know the last grade I got on a test, but I don't do such a good job of recalling the grades on tests before that.

☐ I keep track of all my grades in my course notebooks.

THE IMPORTANCE OF SCOREBOARDS. WHO'S WINNING?

While sitting at a basketball game, I noticed that I was constantly looking up at the scoreboard. After every basket, I would look up to check the score: back and forth from the court to the scoreboard.

Finally, I asked myself why? The score was changing by only two or three points. Why wasn't I just keeping the score in my head and concentrating on the game?

My answer was that checking the scoreboard so often was part of my enjoyment of the game. I wanted to see that my team was really four points ahead, eight points ahead — or sometimes coming up from behind and needing only six points to tie. Seeing that score change was almost as important as watching the ball going through the home team's hoop.

Each semester is like watching several games (courses) with a lot of points (grades).

> ## As with scoreboard watching, you should pay attention to all your grades on tests, quizzes, and assignments — from the beginning of semesters to the end.

True, when grades in a certain class are not very good or dipping, looking at a C (or worse) isn't much fun. But checking your "score" each time you get a grade is very important. It's how you stay involved in all your courses. It's a way of being in control.

ACADEMIC SCOREBOARDS: YOUR COMPETITIVE EDGE

What you need, then, is a scoreboard for each of your classes. Each scoreboard should list all your grades for that class as the semester moves along. That's how you track your progress.

If your grades are generally high (and you're really learning, not cramming), then you're winning the game. You're doing the right things in controlling your courses, your time, and your study. If your grades dip, these low scores tell you something's wrong, and you have to change your game strategy.

Why do you need this information? To be in control. To control a course, you must know the importance of all its graded parts: assignments, projects, labs, tests, quizzes, speeches, and so forth. When you know these things, you see the BIG PICTURE in each course. You'll know how each bit of work you do either adds to or subtracts from your grade.

As I said earlier, most teachers explain their grading methods in the class outline handed out at the start of the semester. By reading this outline, you can see how much each test or assignment counts toward your final grade.

Don't understand something about the grading policy? What do you do? You talk to the teacher. Do it during **The First Two Weeks (Strategy 3)**. Don't forget those **Talking Skills (Strategy 5)**.

KNOW THE GAME RULES.

Once you know how the teacher calculates final grades, you have even more power, and it can prevent mistakes. For example, you won't kid yourself into thinking that your good grade on a quiz that counts 10% of your final grade will offset that poor test grade worth 25% of the final grade.

Your academic scoreboard is a grade diary that you create in each of your class notebooks. You already know that you should have a notebook and folder for every class. That's where you keep all your course information — like your course outlines, notes, assignment sheets, and study summaries.

Your scoreboard, let's call it a **Grade Tracker,** is one of those important items that keep you in control. Make a tracker for each course. It's one of the things you should do during **The First Two Weeks** of the semester.

Here's an example of a **Grade Tracker** that coincides with the course's grade-able items. This particular **Grade Tracker** has five columns.

Quizzes, tests, labs, assignments, etc.	Quiz #1	Paper#1	Report	Mid-Test	Quiz #2	Paper #2	Quiz #3	Final Exam
Grade earned	A	C	B	A	B	B	A	A
%age of final grade	5%	15%	10%	20%	5%	15%	5%	25%
		20% of your class completed		50% of your class completed		70% of your class completed		100%Final grade!

AN AFTER-GAME ANALYSIS: WHAT A GRADE-TRACKER TELLS YOU

- You take your first quiz and get an *A*. Good for you! You were very well prepared.

- Then you write your first paper. You got a *C*. Not so good. What happened here? Didn't you spend enough time on it? Did you misunderstand the assignment? Are writing papers hard for you? For the next paper, you'll have to put more effort into it. Be sure to **talk to your teacher** to find out what was wrong. Get to the root of the problem. Then don't let it happen again on your next paper. And whatever you do, don't just walk away and get discouraged. That's not the way to improve your grade.

- Now you get a *B* on your report. Where are you at this point in the semester? You've completed 30% of your grade. Your grades are up and down. They should be higher and more consistent. At this point, you have somewhere between a *B* and a *C.* So what's your next step? First, find out why you're going up and down — only you know that. Are you studying enough or are you studying only now and then? Are you concentrating? Is this what's happening in all of your classes? You've got to answer all of these questions to do better.

- What you DON'T say is "I'm just not that good in this subject." You could be good if you just improved your study strategies.
- What you DON'T say is "Well I can bring my grade up later." That's a good idea, but how are you going to do it? And when are you going to get started? **Later** is a dangerous word to students.
- What you DON'T say is, *"That B isn't bad."* You might not still have that *B* as the material gets harder. Why do you need an *A*? Why isn't a *B* good enough? Are you college-bound? *Read on.*

So what's your next step? What does your **Grade Tracker** tell you? You've got a midterm coming up! How much does it count? 20% of your final grade. You have to gear-up for this test. And that means figuring out why your grades are so uneven. You want to "fix" what's wrong.

Well now you're doing better. You got an *A* on your midterm. You see — you can do the job when you make the effort and when you use your **Grade Tracker** to understand what it's telling you.

- But what happened after the midterm? On your quiz and paper, you got only *B*s. Did you let that midterm *A* go to your head? Did you get over-confident and not do enough work on the quiz and the paper? Remember: classes get harder as the semester goes on. Did you forget? Your grades slipped. Only 25% of your grade is an *A*. 45% of your grade is less than an *A*. What do you do? Increase your effort. You got an *A* on the midterm, so you can do it again, if you try.
- Bravo! You got an *A* not only on the quiz, but more importantly, on the final exam. You did it! You got a final grade of *A-* even though your grades went up and down. You got high grades on the items that counted the most.

See what you can do with the power of your Grade Tracker! It told you that if you slack off, then you'll fall down. But if you *consistently and regularly* give study time and effort throughout the semester, you've shown yourself that you can earn straight *A*s.

 BE COLLEGE SMART. A grade tracker is a very important tool in college. Why? You'll find that in college, tests and assignments are far fewer than in high school. So each grade counts more. A grade tracker always tells you where you stand. And when you know where you stand, you'll know how to adjust your **Personal Map** in all your courses. See how these two Strategies connect?

Knowing the score tells you how
well you're playing the game.

WHAT YOU NEED TO KNOW ABOUT B GRADES — AND PLUSES AND MINUSES

For a variety of reasons, high school grades are higher than they've ever been. If you're a student who will be applying to college, you should know that college admissions offices are used to seeing *A*s on student records.

Therefore, the difference between an *A* and an *A*- or an *A*- and a *B*+ becomes significant to these reviewers. Quite frankly, *B*s aren't very impressive in the world of college applications these days.

When so many college-bound students have *A*s, college admissions officers must make distinctions. Therefore, pluses and minuses on grades become more significant than ever. *B* grades (or lower) stick out like sore thumbs. This makes grade tracking even more important.

When one test grade lowers your grade average, even in the middle of a course, that's a big deal. You need to start controlling the course and asking yourself, "What do I need to do to turn this around?" Read on.

YOUR EARLY WARNING THAT SOMETHING'S WRONG.

When your **Grade Tracker** signals sliding grades, it's time to find out why. If you're not understanding something in the class, go get help. Talking with your teacher or counselor/adviser about sliding grades is ALWAYS a good thing to do. They can help you understand whatever is giving you trouble.

- Plus, investigate what's going on in your days.
- Maybe your study place needs some renovation.
- Are you getting enough sleep?
- Do you need to revise your **Personal Map?**
- Is more study time in this class the answer?

You're a student all day long. Yes, you have so many other activities and responsibilities. But don't forget your priority list. Make sure studying doesn't slip down on that list. If it is slipping, make sure to keep on pushing it up.

Stay off the "grade roller coaster," which takes you up sometimes and drops you down at others. You're much better off if you apply the Strategies and work steadily and smarter each semester to maintain your grades.

GRADE TRACKERS: YOUR PERSONAL SCOREBOARDS

Keep your **Grade Tracker** in your class notebook. Keep it up to date. Review it often. Pay attention to what it's telling you on a grade-by-grade basis.

6 ways to use your Tracker to control your classes
You'll know....

1. how many grades you have in a class and how each counts toward your final grade.
2. how every bit of work you do either adds or subtracts from your final grade.

3. how to plan your personal activities around studying for upcoming tests, projects, and papers.
4. how to use your **Grade Tracker** to evaluate your study efforts.
5. how well you're in control of the class and your grades.
6. how to make sure that school and studying don't slide down on your priority list.

Remember that kayak we mentioned in the early pages of this book? Tracking prevents you from being swept away by the strong currents — or smashed against the rocks.

LISTEN TO DR. BOB —
Why you need to practice this Strategy for college

In college, grade tracking is hugely important. Why? When your grades become irregular, all of your classes are affected. When all of your classes are affected, you might just let one or more of your classes slide. If that happens, you might have to withdraw from a course to avoid a low grade.

What if this happens several semesters in a row? You could end up with a low overall grade point average. You'll fall behind in your degree requirements. You might have to change your major because you're grades are low. You could find yourself on academic probation. If these things happen, you'll be constantly playing catch-up. In the end, you might have to spend more time in college to get a degree. And what does that mean? You got it. MORE money. Who's paying for this, anyway?

Think about it this way: In middle and high school, you are steered in a direction to make sure that you graduate on time. In college, you have to do your own steering. That's why I used a kayak to make the point. It's up to you to keep track of your requirements as well as your grades. So students who are in control of things graduate in four years, rather than five, six, or more.

But you're going to be college smart. Right? Right.

Think of this book as a map. It's guiding you up the mountain. With each step, you'll move with greater and greater confidence. So keep this map close to you. The heights that you'll have to cover can be downright scary at times. But following your map will get you to where you're going: the summit. What a great view from the top!

UP CLOSE AND PERSONAL

Kyle: He wasn't "watching his weight."

College classes have midterm exams so students know how well they're doing in each class. Kyle came to see me three weeks after his midterms in the first semester of his sophomore year. He was a scholarship student and had to keep a certain grade point average. At midterms, Kyle had three *C*s, a *B*, and a *D* in his classes.

He wanted to talk to me about the *D* in history.

Dr. Bob: How have you done in history since the midterm?

Kyle: Very much better. I got a *B-* on the test last week. Things are coming together.

Dr. Bob: So right now in history, you have two *D*s and a *B-*. Have you figured out what grades you need on your essay assignment and your final exam to get at least a *B* in history? You know you need a *B* average in all your classes to keep your scholarship.

Kyle: Oh, I'll do fine.

Dr. Bob: But tell me, that essay assignment and final exam — how much do they count towards your final grade?

Kyle: Blank stare. (Pause) I don't know.

Dr. Bob: Isn't it on the course outline that you got at the beginning of the semester?

Kyle: Oh, yeah. I've got it in my backpack. Wait. I'll find it. Here it is. It says there are three tests and one written assignment, and then the final. The three tests count 20% each, the essay is 10%, and the final exam is 30%.

Dr. Bob: Okay, let's do the math. You've taken three tests. Your grades were two *D*s and a B-. That means you've completed 60% of your final grade. If the class ended right now, what would your final grade be?

Kyle: I don't know.

Dr. Bob: About a low *C*.

Kyle: I guess, but I know I can bring the grades up. I know what I have to do now.

Dr. Bob: How about dropping the class?

Kyle: No, I dropped English last semester, and if I drop history, too, I'll be really far behind.

At the end of the semester, Kyle got a final grade of B in history. But it took so much effort that he let his other classes slip. His final grades in those were three *C*s and a *D*.

He completely blew his final test in math, which counted 40% of his grade. He lost his scholarship.

DEAN'S COMMENTARY

So, do you see what can happen when you're not following your grades on a **Grade Tracker**? In Kyle's case, not only did he get low grades, he lost his scholarship. If he'd followed the course outline and had used a **Grade Tracker,** *and if he'd seen me after his first low grade,* his life might've been completely different.

There're a lot of students you might know who're like Kyle. So many of my students in trouble were like Kyle: oblivious to grade weights. He didn't read or understand the rules of the class on the course outline, so at various points in the semester, he didn't know where he was in terms of grades. Don't be like Kyle.

So do you see how important your **Grade Tracker** is? From the start of the semester, you know where you are, you know what you have to do, and you know where you have to end up. Knowing all of that will always control your efforts, day by day and week by week, to stay on track towards high final grades.

By now, you've guessed that the plots of these **Up Close and Personal** stories grow out of what I heard in my office day after day. You'll have an edge if you listen well. You'll avoid these problems.

STRATEGY 11

Your college application, extracurricular activities, and recommendations

· ·

Here's where it all comes together: A winning application that stands out. Be sure to read the Up Close & Personal to see how the 12 Strategies shape your application.

NOTE: This Strategy is written not only for college-bound high school students, but also for college graduates applying to graduate, professional, and advanced programs.

This Strategy shows you how all the first 10 Strategies create students valued by prospective schools. Not only do you "have it together personally," but schools will rank you high on their list of candidates.

You choose people as friends because you like them personally and you like the things they do. When selecting students, colleges do the same thing. They want students who are personally outstanding, as well as academically talented.

These days, there are many more applicants than seats at good colleges, so admissions officers can afford to be choosey. Extracurricular activities and letters of recommendation are always important because both tell admissions officers about who you are <u>deep down inside</u> the student. Sound familiar? (p.xvii)

These things may seem unimportant, but they can make a big difference. Most colleges must choose students from applicants with the same high grades and test scores. So extracurricular activities and recommendations can make all the difference.

 LEARN ABOUT YOURSELF

Check those that apply to you.

Note: extracurriculars are all non-classroom activities in and out of school.

When it comes to extracurricular activities, I —

☐ Don't take part in many, and join them only to be with my friends.

☐ Do just a few and give a lot of time to each.

☐ Participate only in activities away from school (part-time jobs, scouting, clubs).

☐ Take part only in activities connected with school (sports, Key Club, Drama Club).

☐ Do only activities that I think will look good on a college application.

☐ Sign up for as many as I can. I hear they're important on a college application.

Activity	Hours Spent Weekly

Your extracurriculars and number of hours per week you spend on each.

ALL THE PARTS TO THINK ABOUT IN CHOOSING A COLLEGE

When you think about choosing, applying to, and enrolling in a college, you should consider these things:

- to get into the best college that you can
- to get into the most affordable college that you can
- to know about the whole application process
- to know if the college offers majors that interest you
- to apply to at least five colleges
- to know why those colleges select some students and not others.
- to understand how your whole pre-college program will look to an admissions officer

Look in the **Bonus section** at the end of the book for information about shopping for and applying to colleges.

As I've said earlier, you're not just a student. You're a whole person. Active, interesting, and intelligent. Remember the chapter on **Who are you deep down—inside and out?** Think about yourself as a student *and a person* applying to college.

How do admissions officers discover that person inside of you? Through extracurriculars (ECAs) and letters of recommendation.

PART 1: WHAT'S AN "ECA"? WHY THEY'RE IMPORTANT.

ECAs (extracurricular activities) cover a wide range of school-related activities, such as athletics, music, forensics, the school newspaper, student government, and the many clubs that your school offers.

Out-of-school activities count, too: scouting, 4-H, church groups, volunteer groups, and, yes, even your part-time job. Anything you do regularly outside of class, anything that takes time, commitment, energy, and intelligence is considered an ECA.

I've told you already that people who evaluate college applications always want to discover who you are as a complete person, not just as a set of grades and SAT or ACT scores. Why is that?

Look at it this way. High grades, test scores, and school awards tell a lot about you — that you are intelligent, diligent, focused, determined, and creative. However, they do not reveal your broader and deeper qualities: your personality or your character.

If people who admit students to good colleges or who award scholarships looked only at transcripts, their decisions would be narrow and even unfair. What's more, their colleges wouldn't be as good as they should be.

BRAIN POWER WITHOUT PERSONALITY AND CHARACTER IS NOT ENOUGH.

True, you definitely develop both personality and character in the classroom, but those qualities are not noticeable just by looking at final grades and GPAs.

That's why admissions officers, scholarship committees, or directors of college honors programs look beyond your grades and test scores to the summary of ECAs you include in your application.

In an ECA summary, students define themselves personally, highlighting qualities like —

- Leadership
- Enthusiasm
- Friendliness
- Responsibility
- Respect for others
- Generosity
- The drive to expand their outlook on life.

ECAs transform you from a black-and-white photo into a colorful video presentation with background music and lively commentary! When a student is applying not only for admission but also for a scholarship or grant award, a strong ECA profile is simply essential.

The student with strong ECAs will always maintain a competitive edge when applying to good colleges. **But always keep in mind: ECAs aren't going to make up for average or inconsistent grades.**

WHAT'S A STRONG ECA?

1. *Strong* doesn't mean that you must sign up for 14 clubs, play a sport every season, work a job 25 hours each week, plus do charity work and run for class president. A packed ECA list will only make you look overwhelmed and rather unbelievable.

With too many ECAs, you obviously can't contribute much time to any single one. Evaluators recognize this immediately, to your disadvantage. And with so many ECAs, someone reviewing your application will ask, "Did this student ever study?"

2. At the other extreme, spending all of your time on one activity, like the school play or a varsity sport, isn't good either.

You're much better off devoting your time to a few varied ECAs, really becoming involved in just a few. That way, college admissions officers will easily recognize the quality of your involvement and dedication, rather than the unbelievable length of your list.

3. One of these ECAs should really stand out, showing that you're truly an exceptional person as a class officer, an athlete, member of the high school band/orchestra, or a leader in a club or organization.

CAREER-RELATED ECAs

If you have a career goal in mind, look for ECAs that relate to that goal.

- If you want to go into medicine, see what kinds of work you can do as a volunteer or summer employee in a hospital or medical center.
- Think you want to go to law school after college? See if a law firm needs a student to help part-time.
- An IT specialist? Look for summer jobs or internships. Learn more about these workplaces. Get experience. See if "they're for you."
- Engineering, government, accounting, finance, journalism, public relations? Ask your parents or family friends if anyone can introduce you to someone working in these fields. Go see these people to find out more about these careers. Just visiting them now and then at their office can give you a great impression of what they do. In the process, you might find yourself a summer job that will give you a great career experience — as well as something you can put on your ECA resumé.

PART 2: WHY RECOMMENDATIONS ARE IMPORTANT

Another way that colleges evaluate the student as a person is to look at letters written by teachers and counselors/advisers who know that student especially well.

Imagine you're applying to a good school right now. Name three teachers, counselors/advisers, or ECA directors who know you well enough *right now* to write a detailed one-page recommendation for you.

1. _____

2. _____

3. _____

Recommendations describe you more fully as a person. They are written by people who know you very well, both in class and out. They are the words of people who see you in comparison with many other students and can describe your remarkable qualities. These letters are an essential part of the application for admission to college. Don't have any good recommenders now? If it's not too late, start using the Strategies.

While many schools want only one recommendation, some really good schools usually want at least two, and even three. No matter how many recommendations you need, each could make a great deal of difference to your gaining admission.

In writing a letter of recommendation, the writer will consider certain qualities that make you stand out, like being —

- Creative
- Articulate (you can talk well on your feet)
- Outgoing
- Communicative (you like to talk)
- Motivated
- Respectful
- Dependable
- Friendly
- Trustworthy
- Generous
- Honest

These are characteristics that people can't see on your transcript, but they're every bit as important.

ABOUT BUILDING RECOMMENDATIONS

Just as you should choose your ECAs carefully and then work to develop them, you should plan ahead for letters of recommendation **long before you actually need them.**

1. You should apply to colleges early in your senior year. Therefore, your recommendations will come from people who know you well by the end of your junior year. A **College Smart Student** gets to know potential recommenders early on, well ahead of the time a recommendation is needed.

2. When the time comes to ask for recommendations, never just hand over a form or a note along with a college address. Make an appointment to see the recommender and talk about your college plans.

3. At the same time, hand over —
    ◊   A detailed summary of your extracurricular activities
    ◊   A copy of your college application essay(s)
    ◊   Your scores on your ACTs, SATs, and AP tests if any
    ◊   A list of the colleges to which you're applying

With this information, a recommender will be able to create a fuller and more detailed recommendation.

If you're a college student applying to a post-graduate program, follow the same procedures as listed here.

WHAT A RECOMMENDATION LETTER LOOKS LIKE

I am delighted to recommend Eric Washburn for admission to Oberlin College. I've been a teacher of English for 20 years at Brookfield East High School, one of the highest-ranked public schools in Wisconsin. More of our students score 4 or 5 on AP tests than any other school in the state. Our graduates are regularly accepted at elite colleges and universities each year.

As a teacher and recommender, I want to brag a little by mentioning that I was given a Teacher of the Year award (2012) for our school district.

As a junior in my AP class, Eric was always at the center of the action — one of those students who naturally generates excitement in a class. Daily, he made insightful comments and asked provocative questions, showing he was always in the moment. I think his classmates learned as much from him as from me! My colleagues all say the same thing: "He's one of a kind."

Eric's such a personable guy that his classmates obviously like and respect him. I've seen it so many times while just walking by him in the hall. He's always cheerful, always friendly, always considerate of others. And he has a great sense of humor. When he's around, you're always smiling or laughing. He has a bright outlook on life.

When he asked me for this recommendation, he made an appointment to see me and brought in his completed application to your college. Very few students come to me so organized. Looking at his list of extracurricular activities, I saw they were a reflection of Eric as a whole person. I knew he was a star on the tennis team, but I learned he was also the captain. Not bad on the cross-country team, either. I didn't know he was president of the Key Club and a tutor for students in freshman math. Plus, he volunteers in the community, too.

Eric really wants to enroll in Oberlin. He wants a small liberal arts college with a national reputation. He tells me he has visited your campus twice. He tells me he's serious about your school. He has yet to decide on a major. He writes with such originality and elegance, he could be a writer of anything from fiction to who knows what. What he does is always done brilliantly. He wrote an essay for me on Dickens' *Tale of Two Cities* that was so well done, I still keep it in my desk drawer as a sample of excellence. Maybe it will work as a lucky charm and attract more students like Eric to my courses in the future.

Having written so many recommendations over the years, I've come to judge a student's quality in terms of my years teaching: for example, "the best students in my class this year;" "the best student in my class in the last two years," and so forth. Eric is clearly the best student I've had in five years. Students, like Eric, whom I've recommended in the past, have graduated from schools like Yale, Washington University, Stanford, MIT, and the University of Chicago.

Eric is a perfect student for Oberlin, just as he was a perfect student in Brookfield East. He's also applying to Amherst and Grinnell, so you don't want to wait around too long on your decision!!!!

Sincerely,

Finally, don't let anyone tell you that recommendations and ECAs are *"not that important – nobody looks at them anyway."* Even if admissions officers ignore them, that's not your concern. Your concern is to submit the most complete application that you can.

When admissions officers examine ECAs and recommendations, this background can make all the difference in the decision-making process. When you want to get into the colleges that seem just right for you, never be careless about your applications or the details and procedures they require.

How else can colleges learn more about you? When you visit these schools! It's something you should do before you apply. Colleges like to see interested students face to face.

Admissions officers often record their impressions of visiting students. Use your talking skills to impress anyone you talk to when you visit a college! These notes then become part of your application. Students who can talk are impressive. Your parents shouldn't do all the talking.

Be sure to visit the colleges twice that you know you're going to apply to.

LISTEN TO DR. BOB —
What you should know about Admissions Applications

What will make your application stand out?

- **High standardized test scores.** Make sure you prepare for these tests. They're really important.

- **Extracurricular activities.** They should be impressive, but few.

- **Recommendations.** Ask anyone who knows you well enough — usually teachers and counselors/advisers or employers — to write strong, detailed letters for you.

- **Visit colleges early. Look at a few, not just one. (See my BONUS offering at the end of the book.)**

- **Apply early — in October.**

Don't use Internet services to "help you" with your College Application Essay.

First of all, it's dishonest, thereby making your application fraudulent. Colleges want to read an essay created and composed by you personally. When an Internet source says it will "help you," that usually means they'll write it for you or come very close to doing it.

Second, if somehow a college admissions officer believes your letter is unauthentic — or even suspects that it is — your application will end up on the Denied pile. Then, you'll get a letter of rejection, and you'll never know if it was because you submitted a suspicious essay, written by an Internet Service.

Third, just don't do it. It's too risky.

 UP CLOSE AND PERSONAL

I'm talking directly to YOU now.

Do you see how all the Strategies are related to the characteristics that colleges value? You'll be —

- self-reliant
- a forward-looking person
- an organized, independent learner
- an active participant in courses
- a well-rounded person in and out of school
- a person who values learning as a way of choosing a future
- an interesting human being who is aware of the future and focused on getting there and succeeding
- a contributor, a fine addition to any campus
- a graduate the college/university would be proud of

In short, this book gives you a detailed road map for admission to a quality college/university. Just being smart isn't enough.

Sara: What her recommendation didn't say.

Remember Sara from **Strategy 4**? She had perfect ACT scores and ranked #1 in her class, but she couldn't get passed admissions interviews for the nation's most-prized colleges.

Not being able to speak well hurt her, and because her recommendations were neutral, they disqualified her, too. Let me explain.

At my university, I worked closely with the Admissions Office, so I looked at student applications almost daily. When university officers review recommendations, they look at what is written — *and what is not written.*

Neutral letters will say something like, *"While I do not know this student personally, she was in my class and earned a [letter grade]."*

Such language tells admissions counselors that this is a passive student who, after three years in high school and many teachers, cannot produce a truly personal letter of recommendation.

What the letter actually says is that this student may have earned high grades but failed to stand out from other students.

In other words, what the teacher DIDN'T say was a story in itself.

Colleges wanted to hear that Sara not only was bright and capable but also actively participated in discussions ... that she made the class more interesting for other students ... and that the class was better because she was in it.

Sara's teachers said none of these things. When teachers write recommendations, they praise students wherever possible because teachers know colleges are interested in that kind of personal information.

When colleges looked at Sara's letters of recommendation, they saw what was missing. Sara's grades, class rank, and test scores were excellent. But the people who looked at her application couldn't see the "person deep down inside the student." At their college, they wanted to enroll interesting people as well as excellent students.

⤺ DEAN'S COMMENTARY

As a **College Smart Student,** that won't happen to you. You have already built a relationship with your recommender, **by talking to teachers,** so he or she can speak specifically about you as a person. Want to know what else?

> **Your recommenders can write about—**
> - your **special interest** in a particular course
> - your **leadership in class** discussions

- your care in following a **Personal Map**
- your **well-organized approach** to school
- your **motivation to learn and contribute**
- your **great work**
- **your serious drive to succeed** with your education
- your **personal growth** developed through your ECAs

Think about your current ECAs. Think about your relationships with your teachers, and advisers. How many of them do you know well enough to write you a terrific letter of recommendation? Now that you know the kinds of qualities you need for a strong letter of recommendation, practice them.

ARE YOU HEARING ANY BELLS RINGING?

Do all of these qualities sound like things you've heard in earlier Strategies? Of course.

> Is it all starting to come together for you? Are you beginning to see how the Strategies work for you on many levels?

Finally, it's true that some colleges might not care much about the recommendations they request — they may use them only when making difficult admissions decisions. You never know exactly how colleges evaluate your application.

But you must treat recommendations and extracurriculars as counting significantly in the admissions process. You don't know what role they will play for you. So as far as you're concerned, believe that they are as important as grades and test scores, and give them the attention they require.

ABOUT EXTRACURRICULARS

They enable you to grow as a person. If you can organize a fund-raiser, coordinate an event, take responsibility in student government, and so forth, you are showing your abilities.

You can organize, you take initiative, you're responsible, meet deadlines, and see things through to their end. **You show that you are an interested, active, energetic, can-do person.** These are accomplishments you can talk about in a job interview to demonstrate your experiences. If you have had internships or summer jobs, you have experience. Think like an employer. What are they looking for? **Proof of your abilities to get things done.**

You're really interested in learning.

- Your attitude? Education is important, a preparation for college and life.
- You understand your education develops you personally as well as academically.
- You're in control of your life as a student.
  - ◊ You're always prepared for class, tests, & assignments.
  - ◊ You get high grades.
  - ◊ You contribute to class discussions.
  - ◊ You've established relationships with your teachers.
  - ◊ You act independently and take initiative to manage your studies.
- You show a remarkable personality and character.
- You prepare for standardized tests.
- You take challenging courses, like Advanced Placement.
- You take four years, rather than three, of foreign language, math, and science.

Do you see how the 11 strategies so far all combine to give you an edge in the admissions process?

STRATEGY 12

Setting goals — *getting to the top. What a view!*

• •

Making your dreams and hopes come true.

In a survey, new college freshmen were asked to comment on how interesting they found their last year of high school. Almost half said they were "frequently bored." In this Strategy, I'm going to tell you things that will really open your eyes. I'm telling you these things so you can avoid them. One of the reasons I wrote this book is that I don't want them happening to you. I wrote the book to reverse these trends.

Only 37% (about 1 in 3) of college students complete a degree in four years. College students who take longer to finish degrees, spend more and more money and get way over their heads in debt.

25% of college freshmen do not return to the college where they started (or do not return to school at all).

40% of students arrive at college needing remedial work. 25% of these students need "substantial" help — many in several subjects.

Almost 40% of college students don't have a degree after six years. Many never expected this to happen.

And the statistics about students **in community colleges are, regrettably, even worse.**

Boredom, disinterest, and apathy seriously harm students at all levels of education. Follow this Strategy, and I promise this won't happen to you.

PART 1: NEVER BE BORED WITH SCHOOL AGAIN!

How about you? Do you find school boring? Don't you wish you could jump over school and just start your life? Here's how to add interest, challenge, and enthusiasm to what you might consider your "dreary and monotonous" school days.

Begin by bringing to school a sense of your FUTURE. You link your school days to your special goals: what you might like to "be" or a career you might want to follow.

Don't say, "Here's another boring Tuesday." Tuesday — and every other day in school — connects you to your future.

WHERE THE BOREDOM COMES FROM

In grade school, you didn't have to set goals. Your teachers set them for you, telling you exactly what to do.

- "Today we are going to listen carefully to the story, so we can answer questions later."
- "This afternoon, we are going to practice writing neatly."
- "Now, we're going to play a game to prepare for tomorrow's test."

Elementary school was a time of close teacher-student relationships. Teachers made learning exciting. They helped and encouraged you. They helped you learn in class, not outside of class. Your teacher moved from student to student, either congratulating each on a job well done or helping each student understand the lesson.

In middle school, that close teacher-student relationship changed.

You had several teachers, and you moved from classroom to classroom. Teachers spent most of class time explaining concepts, not working with you.

To succeed, you had to set your own goals. It was up to you to make the effort to reach them. What kind of goals? Here are a few:

- coming to class prepared
- paying attention in class
- studying and completing homework thoughtfully
- handing in assignments on time
- preparing for tests
- contributing to class discussions
- showing a genuine interest in the subject
- relating to teachers in a new way

Without your teachers' individual attention and support, you may have found that some subjects became harder for you than others. You may have found yourself on your own, wrestling with them. Your first thought may have been just to give up.

Sooner or later, you realized that school expected more from you independently. You were growing up, and it was up to you to take control of your education. Part of the growing up process in school is learning that not everything comes easily. Go back to the athlete model. You have to encourage yourself, saying,

"I know math is tough for me, so I'll have to work harder to get it."

"It's difficult doing all this reading and writing, but I'll stick with it."

In middle school, for some students, this worked. For others, it didn't. If it didn't, the thing to do was to ask for help — to use your initiative to talk to the teacher. And if you did, you saw the results in higher grades and discovered that teachers like to help you.

THE PROBLEM WITH GIVING UP (THE TROUBLE DOESN'T GO AWAY)

No matter where you are in school — middle school, high school, or college — when you discover a subject that's "hard" for you, don't give up on it! Don't say:

- "The subject is *dumb* or *useless*."
- "I just don't like it."
- "I don't need it. I'll never use this stuff."
- "It's boring."

These kinds of students don't ask themselves the questions, "*Why is it boring? Why don't I like it? Why is it useless?*" They were too *boorrred* to ask the questions. So what happens?

They begin to fall behind in the class
because they don't work at it.

They don't pay attention in class because now
they can't follow what the teacher is saying.

The subject becomes even harder as the weeks move on.

Their *boredom* increases, along with their frustration and anger.

Students give up on the subject. They think they
can avoid taking more classes in this subject. But
they don't have this choice. Here's why.

Get a low grade this semester in an English class, and next semester, English will be even harder for you. Give up on English in high school, and college English will be impossible for you. The same with math, sciences, *etc.* This applies to all your subjects.

Get low grades in different classes, and you harm your whole education, at any level. These gaps in your education build up and eventually undermine everything — high school, college, and even career. In short, boredom wrecks your future.

Giving up on a subject affects not just your
grades and your attitude toward school, but your
entire future. Don't believe it? Read on!

THINK VERY LONG-TERM.

This giving-up-on-learning-certain-things attitude will wreck your future. But you don't know it yet. By the time you understand this, it'll be too late.

- When you give up on a hard subject, **you lock doors to college majors and careers** — some you haven't even thought about yet. You won't be able to take the courses you need to get those jobs. And if you do manage to get a job, you won't be able to perform at the level expected.
- You'll also have set a terrible pattern of behavior for yourself. **When something is hard, you don't do it.** Can you imagine the reaction when you say to a future boss, "I'm not good at that — you better give the project to someone else."

Without the ability and courage to set and achieve new goals each day of your life, you cannot grow and evolve. Don't think only for the moment. Think long-term.

HARD SUBJECT — HARD GAME

What if you looked at a hard subject the way athletes look at the challenge of competition? Athletes work hard to achieve excellence, and they're proud of their hard work and accomplishments. For them, learning new things or sharpening their skills is exciting.

As a student, imitate athletes. You'll feel a sense of accomplishment because you *conquered* something that wasn't easy for you. **You'll be a winner.**

Oprah says: "The big secret in life is that there is no big secret. Whatever your goal, you can get there only if you are willing to work."

BEWARE THE LEFT-BRAIN/RIGHT-BRAIN TRAP.

Often people conclude that being "left-brained" or "right-brained" blocks learning certain subjects. Not true.

The truth is that the right/left-brain theory refers only to a person's style or manner of learning, *not the ability to learn.* There's no reason that the left-brained student can't learn right-brained subjects, or the reverse.

BALANCE IS THE NAME OF THE GAME.

When students simply give up on one type of academic subject, they weaken their overall strength. Want some examples?

- What if a brilliant engineer can't write or speak very well? When people don't really understand the work or its value to them, the engineer has failed in the final step to get people to buy or appreciate his work. The idea won't go very far. No matter how brilliant he/she may be, the engineer is going to have a tough time going anywhere in the profession.

- The journalist who can't understand economics, statistics, or matters of science will limit what he or she can write about. They'll wind up writing on only a few topics. They won't go far either.

Work hard for balanced and broad knowledge. Learn about a lot of different areas: from science to art, from math to English, from history to social sciences.

BALANCE MAKES LEARNING WORK.

From one level of education to another, you have to balance your effort in all your subjects. You can't afford to label any one of them as *boring*. You can't decide to work hard in some classes, and let others slide. You'll have to take them again in college. They'll be much harder and you won't be ready to handle them.

In college, even though you can choose a major as a focus, you'll still have to take a variety of other subjects to complete your degree, *most of them, the same subjects you took in high school.* So, to manage all the subjects required for your degree, you have to begin college with a balanced education.

PART 2: GOALS FOR YOUR FUTURE

LEARN ABOUT YOURSELF

Are you a goal setter?

Check any that apply to you.

☐ I set some goals, but I don't know if they're the right ones.

☐ No, I live from day to day. Life's too unpredictable.

☐ I set goals, but I don't usually keep them. They fizzle out.

☐ I'm a goal-setter from way back. Goals keep me on track.

☐ I always tell myself, "This year, I'll do better." That's a goal, isn't it?

☐ I like calendars. I like to know what's coming up for me.

PLANNING FOR YOUR FUTURE?

Whether or not you have goals from day to day, semester to semester, or year to year, what about the BIG GOAL — a career? Check any that apply to you.

☐ I think about my future, mostly daydreams filled with huge successes.

☐ I believe that things always work out, right?

☐ A few careers interest me, but I don't know much about them.

☐ I talk regularly to my teachers and counselors about colleges, careers, and jobs.

☐ It's all so scary right now. I'm just avoiding it. I'll think about it later.

☐ Whenever I meet an adult, I ask about what they do for a living.

DREAMS, HOPES, STRATEGIES, GOALS: KNOW THE DIFFERENCE.

Some students focus only on their distant goals.

- I want to be a famous architect who designs buildings that last forever.
- I want to own a big company and have a lot of people working for me.
- I want to be a millionaire — earn a fortune at an early age and not worry about the rest of my life.

These are dreams. We all need them. But don't mistake dreams for goals. Successful people will tell you that the most important part of reaching your dreams is setting goals and creating the strategies and plans to achieve them.

You have to understand that hopes, dreams, strategies, and goals are like the strands of a rope. They all work together. But the strands are separate. So you must untwist the strands and understand them separately.

- **Dreams show you your destination.** I dream of working for Microsoft.
- **Hopes are your motivation.** I'll work hard to become an innovative computer engineer.
- **Strategies are the *how* steps that get you to your goals.** I'll excel in all my courses so that I'll be accepted into a really great engineering school. I'll get there by setting and meeting lots and lots of short-term goals all along the way.

GETTING FROM HERE TO THE END OF THE SEMESTER

Let's bring this down to a smaller level. When I ask students to name some goals for a new semester, the first thing most students say is "to get high final grades." "To procrastinate less" comes in a close second.

But how do you "get" those high final grades? What keeps you going from day to day? Smaller, specific goals that you can easily control, check-off, and evaluate every day. The idea is to work in small chunks each day. **These smaller chunks are called short-term goals.**

For example:

- Follow your **Map** every day.
- Track your time so you don't waste it.
- Stay organized in your daily life.
- Keep a calendar. Look ahead. Know what's coming next. You don't want surprises.

Short-term goals get you to your long-term goals. Aha! Looking at the list above, this statement may seem obvious right here and now. Yet students often lose sight of the connection between the two kinds of goals. Here's what I mean:

- If you don't do your daily jobs (short-term goals), you won't achieve your long-term goal (becoming a computer engineer).
- On the other hand, if you don't keep your larger purpose (your long-term career goal) clear in your mind, you can lose your willpower to do your daily jobs as a student.

BE COLLEGE SMART. Because short-term goals achieve long-term goals, every time you meet Tuesday's goals or Friday's goals, you're going places. These hundreds of small acts you do in school/college over the years enable you to reach the big long-term goal that is your life: a career that fulfills all your dreams — income, house, family. All those things you want.

ARE YOU AFRAID OF SETTING GOALS? WHY YOU SHOULDN'T BE.

Setting long-term goals, like college majors and careers can be scary. Why? There are so many to choose from. But sooner or later you have to. So start making choices as soon as you can, even though you may change your mind a couple of times. Fear of failing keeps lots of students from setting important goals. Do it. A lot of people will help you — from your teachers, to your counselors to your parents. Just use your talking skills.

Know this about any goals from the start:

- You'll reach some goals more easily than others.
- You won't always succeed the first time. Most strategies have to be adjusted as you go along, and you may find yourself trying different ways to reach those goals.
- If you don't try, nothing ever happens. You'll just be stuck in neutral.
- You have great freedom — you can change your mind, you can change your strategies to succeed, you can even change your outlook on life.
- But sooner or later, you'll have to make some decisions. As a **College Smart Student,** you'll be able to do just that — with great confidence and satisfaction.

LEARN ABOUT YOURSELF

List some important long-term goals for yourself, everything from college to career, and everything in between. Be as specific as you can.

1. _____

2. _____

3. _____

4. _____

SETTING AND REACHING GOALS: A SKILL YOU'LL NEED THROUGHOUT LIFE

You must make reaching goals part of your regular personal routine. If you don't start practicing now, you won't understand how to do it later.

Remember when I told you earlier that learning *how* to learn is as important as *what* you learn? A major part of that *how* is setting and achieving goals.

The What	The How
Get higher grades	Study more and better
Get healthy	Eat less junk food and more veggies
Know more about world events	Keep up with national and world news
Lower stress	Take a yoga class
Get more organized	Clean your room

See how life goals help your school goals and vice-versa? That's why my **12 Strategies** fit so well as great climbing boots: They give you the *hows* of reaching many goals that get you to your personal summit. More on that at the end of this chapter.

FROM HIGH SCHOOL TO COLLEGE TO CAREER

When you're in middle school, you want to think about the challenges of high school. In high school, you should be thinking about the challenges of college. Then in college, you're thinking about where your college education will take you.

Just like climbing the mountain, one level of school always steps up to another level. Think about it this way:

- Many college courses require long papers. If you take high school courses that require writing long essays or papers, that gives you a great advantage. You'll be better prepared for this college work.
- Many colleges require competence in a foreign language. If you do well in your middle and high school foreign language classes, you'll meet your competency requirements in college.
- Many colleges set a standard for math ability. Plus, many college courses require math or computer competence. Take lots of math in high school, so you don't have problems in college work.

Did you ever realize that each day, week, semester, and year has so much to do with what's just around the corner in your life? That's why setting both short- and long-term goals is essential, not just important. **College Smart Students,** like you, will remember this each day.

GRADUATE FROM COLLEGE ON TIME. IT'S A VERY IMPORTANT GOAL.

If you follow my **12 Strategies,** you'll be really ready for college. You'll —

- Love it and find it exciting
- Won't feel stressed in college courses
- Set important goals for yourself
- Get the most out of your college education, both in and out of the classroom
- Appreciate college as a launching pad for a career
- Graduate on time, saving huge amounts of money.

That's exactly what you want to do because college is very expensive, as you know. Remind yourself about how much college costs you and your family. Yes, it's definitely worth the investment, but you don't want to spend more money than you planned to.

Most community college programs are designed to be completed in two years; other colleges, in four years. You don't want to go beyond the normal two or four years because this will turn your expensive college education into a mound of debt.

So you **now** understand how important my Strategies are.

YOUR EDUCATIONAL MOUNTAIN — THE MT. EVEREST OF KNOWLEDGE AND PERSONAL GROWTH

Unlike floating lazily on a raft in a pool, mountain climbing/learning is not something to be taken casually. Being a climber/learner can be very thrilling, but you must stay alert at all times. The climb gets harder as the mountain grows steeper. If you're a **College Smart Student,** each new part of your journey prepares you for the next.

All along the way, you're busy setting short-term goals for yourself to get to the next stage up the mountain. You're continually growing and preparing for the next stage of your climb. You must keep developing as a student. You cannot afford to be careless or bored.

All throughout your school life, you're being asked to act more independently and develop strength. You do that by using the **12 Strategies.** They show you how to achieve your daily and long-term goals. They're your map and plan for the ascent:

- Every class is important. Come to class in "processing mode." *Strategies #1 and 2*
- Study requires time and effort. *Strategies #2, 3, and 7*
- Controlling your time means mapping it out. *Strategy #8*
- Time should be used productively: you have many things to do and only so many hours in a day. *Strategies #2 and 8*
- Talking makes you independent, involves you in the learning process, and earns you good recommendations. *Strategies #4, 5, 6, and 11*
- Evaluating your progress shows how well you're studying in each class. *Strategies #9 and 10*

- Tracking grades tells you when to adjust your **Personal Map**. *Strategy #10*
- Extracurricular activities help you develop and contribute to your college application process. *Strategy #11*
- Strong letters of recommendation play a key role in your college application. *Strategy11*
- How the first 11 Strategies fit together and give you a keen advantage in the College Admissions Process — and a way to Succeed in College. That's why they're important. Getting "into" college is one thing. Succeeding once you're there is quite another.
- Goals keep you moving forward. *Strategy #12*

Use my book and review it often throughout school to remind yourself of what you should be doing. Keep it in your backpack or study place. Pull it out when you're talking to your counselor/adviser.

YOU CAN GET TO THE SUMMIT!

Set goals. Plan how to get there. Do the work. Stick to your plan — adjust it as needed. Don't give up. You're in control. This is your life. **And you're in charge of it. So take charge of it. You can do this.**

Remember all that independence and control you're looking for? You have it. As the **College Smart Climber,** you're creating footholds, planting your axe, staying alert to changing conditions, and choosing the right path to reach the summit. **You can do it!**

Take courses of "substance" and remember what you learn. You want to choose a career that's exciting to you, not *settle* for one because you haven't taken the right courses for a career you might really want. So always take the most challenging courses you can, wherever you are in school.

College is a big goal in your life right now. Place it right in front of you, and work on it every day.

College Smart Students are students with drive. Remember the word, "dynamic," from the early pages of the book? Now you really know what it means.

Dynamic students are interesting people. They're talented and creative. They discover new challenges, fresh excitement, and opportunities to grow. The key is setting and achieving goals and by using the **12 Strategies** to make your dreams and hopes come true.

This is your future!

LISTEN TO DR. BOB —
I want you to be a successful student. I want you to succeed in school. I've talked with so many college students over the years that I know how some students succeed and some don't. What makes the difference? Learning and developing the **12 Strategies** in this book.

If you were in my classroom, we would learn each Strategy week by week. But this isn't a classroom. You have to be your own teacher as well as the student. So study the book and re-read the Strategies. Your goal is to understand how to be a successful student. The course starts now. You have what you need to do the job. **So do it! You're in control.**

Carry this book with you during each stage of school. Think of it as your Wikipedia for learning.

UP CLOSE AND PERSONAL

(Your name), a College Smart Student

In previous Strategies, I've told you stories, "up close and personal." This last story is about you. As a **College Smart Student,** each day you make the most of the Strategies that I've described in this book.

Because you're college smart, you really feel in control. Each day is exciting. Each day is filled with interesting challenges — you like them and you're confident of your success.

You've worked hard to be the kind of student you are. Plus, you continue to work harder each day because you know that you'll be a student for the rest of your life: always learning new things, always solving problems, always creating ways to better understand and manage your career and your life and your many roles in it.

For you, school is practice for life, and when you get there, that's a "contest" you want to win.

Today is a typical day for you. In the morning, after a good night's sleep and breakfast, you look at your **Personal Map** to remind yourself of the things you have to do today. Let's see.

You have a quiz in math — you're ready for that.

You have a paper due in two days in English: you worked on it again last night.

You're up to date on your Spanish vocabulary and tense endings.

You're really looking forward to a new biology lab experiment. You did extra reading for that.

Yes, you're ready for a presentation in your history class.

You're more than ready to face the day.

Looking ahead to your week, you don't want to forget about your appointment with your counselor/adviser. In this appointment, you talk about what you've accomplished so far and if you have any problems. Having somebody to talk to, to bounce ideas off, helps you appreciate the good decisions you've made since the last appointment.

As you head for your first class, you think about the new material to be presented that day. As always, you've read ahead, so you're prepared. In the classroom, you head for your favorite seat, right up front in the second row, so that your eyes and mind always stay focused on your teacher.

Before class begins, you say "hi" to your friends, and then as the class settles, you scan the notes you wrote last night as you read the textbook. Flipping through the pages of your notebook, you notice your **Grade Tracker** for this course. Nice to see those high grades. It's just the boost you need to focus on today's class.

During class, you take notes and ask questions and contribute to class discussions. The teacher appreciates you, and so do the other students, because you ask good questions that they might be reluctant to ask.

After class, you ask your teacher about an upcoming assignment. You do this without hesitation because you talk to all your teachers regularly. You learned long ago that communication is one of the keys to your success as a student. You know that exchanging ideas is what learning is all about.

As you move from class to class, you feel "pumped" because new ideas and concepts get your mind going. Learning feels great. Other students are always complaining, some are even your friends. *"I totally hate that class." "Man, is he ever boring." "I can't wait to get out of my last class and forget about all this stuff tonight."* Well, everyone has opinions; you just prefer being optimistic.

You're already thinking about working ahead. You weren't always like this until you learned how to make a **Personal Study Map**. Now that you've blocked out study time as well as personal time, you find you can do everything: from studying to the other stuff that you like to do.

An important part of your personal time is keeping in shape because that keeps your mind sharp. You're careful about getting exercise and sleep — and not eating too much junk food. You work as a volunteer one Sunday a month, and you sit on two committees. Bored? You don't know the meaning of the word.

You watch other students who do everything haphazardly: no direction, no goals. You've noticed they study less and less yet complain about being overworked more and more. They all need **Personal Maps!**

For you, there's nothing like your study place. Here, no one disturbs you. Everyone you know has learned to respect your study time. You're away from the noise and commotion. You're unplugged!

Each day, you study for all of your classes. You read and re-read carefully highlighting important details. You review old material and read ahead. Your notebooks are an academic diary where you record everything: class notes, outlines of textbook chapters, memory charts, and lists.

Finally, when your day ends, you have a great sense of accomplishment. You're another day closer to your future — career and beyond. Every day is great. You feel great. Your family and friends are proud of you. You're really College Smart.

A DAY IN THE LIFE OF A COLLEGE SMART STUDENT. THE BIG RECAP.

As you come to the end of this book, I hope you understand how important it is to start practicing the **12 Strategies** NOW, not later. Whether you are four years or four weeks away from college, whether you're starting a new semester or in the middle of one, your primary goal should be to make these Strategies a regular part of your days. Remember, we're talking about your future now, and nothing should stand in the way of realizing that future.

I want you to imagine yourself as a **College Smart Student**. What makes you college smart? Here are the essentials.

You keep your goals in mind. When? At the start of each semester. At the start of each new course. In fact, at the start of each new school day, you're thinking about goals — small and big. Every quiz grade, every final grade, every grade point average signals that you're learning more and more, better and better. As a student preparing for college, you can say, "I'm college smart. I reach my goals."

If you're not in college yet, you're setting larger college-related goals (where to go and why). You want to absolutely choose the campus that's right for you.

You manage your time. You design your **Personal Map** during the first two weeks of the semester, calculating hours and putting subjects in order. You've examined your course outlines and reviewed all the course materials, so you know what you need to do each week. You follow your schedule, you study every course every day, and you put in all your hours. You keep copies of your **Personal Map** in the side pockets of your notebooks — and one on the fridge to remind your family when they shouldn't disturb you.

You understand that your **Personal Map** is your best defense against procrastination. *Procrastination kills* (especially students)! It's a good motto. You should post a sign with this motto on the bulletin board in your room. Write it on the covers of your notebooks.

You're organized. You keep course outlines and copies of your **Grade Tracker** in the pockets of your notebooks. These are the tools you use to manage each course. Because you review these pages regularly, you know what your teachers will cover each day; when tests are scheduled; when assignments are due; where you stand in each course; and that you have built time to study into your days.

You're productive. You have a well equipped, quiet place to study, and everyone knows you shouldn't be interrupted during your scheduled study hours. Naturally, you don't take phone calls while you're studying, and you use your computer solely for school work during study time. You stay as far away from distractions as possible.

You check on progress. At the end of every day, you make sure your homework assignments are done and you have studied all your courses. You stay caught up and ahead of your course schedules. You record all your grades in your **Grade Tracker.**

You understand your opportunities. For you, school is invigorating. It gives you the chance to learn something NEW each day. You can see the big picture, and you've started making connections between courses. You view your education as a challenge, much like a competitive sport or playing a musical instrument. You're determined to play at a professional level — and win!

True, school has a strong social side to it, but it is not *only* a social place. It is your job. That means you respect your teachers, even the unpopular ones, and you respect your courses, even when they aren't your favorites. You're open-minded enough to go to school each day saying to yourself, "All this is important for me, even in ways I don't yet understand."

Being college smart is an attitude. *You value your education for what it can do for you* — in college and throughout your life. It is a privilege given to you so you can build your future.

You're ready. And as you go to your first class of the day, you've done the reading or solved the problems, or memorized the vocabulary that prepares you for this class and all of your classes. You've carefully done your homework because you know that your work signals your intellectual growth. You feel the same way about tests.

Ten minutes before class ends, the teacher says very casually, "How about a quiz?" No worries. You're ready.

You're involved. Class begins, and you have your notebook in front of you. You learned a long time ago that notebooks are as important as textbooks, so you take good notes. You also know that keeping a complete notebook for each course is fundamental to your success. Your note-taking helps both your writing and thinking skills.

As you leaf through your notebook pages, your rough class notes are followed by rewritten notes, followed by outlines of textbook chapters. You've arranged important items that need to be memorized in different kinds of charts and lists (along with memory notes to help you fix them in your mind).

You've found a good place to sit in class. You try to stay away from your friends who tend to talk too much.

You contribute. You've discovered that when students come to class prepared, listen, and participate, the class is livelier, more enjoyable, and you learn more. Because you've kept up with your reading and notes, you are always ready to join the discussion. You find you like being involved, contributing your thoughts, hearing what other students have to say, and getting your teacher's reaction. It's an energizing way to learn, and a way to practice talking in front of people.

You're connected. You've got a good working relationship with your teachers because you've made it a point to talk to them. You know that if a course becomes difficult, they are going to help you in or out of the classroom. You can always go to them about study advice, too. As you are packing up to leave class, you ask your teacher a question you've been thinking about. The teacher tells you to stop by after school for a few minutes. No problem. You always discover interesting things when you talk with teachers. In fact, you appreciate the time teachers give you. You found out long ago that talking to teachers makes even the less-interesting classes (and teachers, for that matter) more thought-provoking. And isn't that what you want from every class? Mental excitement!

You're growing. As you walk to your next class and talk to your friends, you can actually feel that you've just energized your mind. It happens every time you are in a learning mode. And perhaps the most important thing you are realizing about your mind: It grows as it processes knowledge, just as a tree processes sunlight, water, and nutrients. Long ago, you stopped thinking of your head as a container into which information is poured.

You know how to succeed. That's why you're a **College Smart Student**. Your great success didn't come naturally any more than playing a sport or an instrument. And you can't wait to get to college. You'll know how to use all of the College Smart Strategies to succeed.

As a college student, with the skill and confidence of an expert learner, you know that you will discover the right career path.

When you're college smart, your life always looks and feels great!

What you want to do may be a goal. But knowing what you want to do won't get you there. You need to have a *how* strategy. Here are some examples to help you get the point:

- *What:* Discover a career is one of my major long-term goals.
- *How:* Taking a career-interest test, meeting someone who works in my field of interest, or interning in an organization that might point me in the right direction and help me get there.

- *What:* Raise my grade in history.
- *How:* Increase the amount of time I give history in my **Map** and talk to my teacher to get pointers.
- *What:* Improve my talking skills.
- *How:* Make a serious effort to talk to different kinds of people.
- *What:* Master the **12 Strategies**.
- *How:* Add at least one new Strategy to my routine each week until I've added them all. I'll begin right NOW! And get really good at them.

So learning is the *how* in meeting goals. We know now that short-term goals achieve long-term goals. **So, every time you meet Tuesday's goal or Friday's goal, you're going places.** These small goals are bringing you closer to a more distant place: your future.

Your job is to stay on target to achieve your dreams! Say it out loud: "I stay on target to achieve my dreams!"

FINAL NOTES: TWO COMMENTS ON TWO SERIOUS TOPICS

Plagiarism — handing in someone else's work

● ●

I magine that you work long and hard on a 15-page research paper on an analysis of George Washington's presidency for your American History course. You get an *A+*. What a feeling of accomplishment!

Then, next semester, you find out that, without your knowing it, another student has gotten your paper and used your hard work for an assignment in American Politics. How would you feel? Would you feel betrayed, cheated, "robbed?"

Yes! While you weren't robbed of money or other valuables, the other student stole your thoughts, your time, and your hard work. The other student is guilty of a type of academic cheating called *plagiarism*.

Plagiarism is taking someone else's thoughts and words and using them as your own.

In our example, it doesn't matter how your *A+* paper was used. The student might have turned in your entire paper with his or her name on it. Maybe the student used only part of your work for a shorter assignment — or delivered your paper for an oral report.

What if the other student didn't use your words exactly — just used your thoughts and analysis? It doesn't make any difference. If your paper was used by someone else in any way without your permission, it is still plagiarism.

It's the same thing if you buy a paper on the Internet. That's plagiarism.

Professors have gotten smarter in detecting plagiarism (and cheating on tests). It's foolish to think there's no risk involved. So what happens when you get caught? That depends on the rules of the college.

Every college writes out their standards and penalties for this kind of unethical behavior. In many colleges, the instance of dishonesty can be become part of your permanent record. That means a single incident can follow you through your life. What impression would it make on an employer who reviews your college transcript to see what kind of student you were? Transcripts are indicators of how well you work in classes and how well you succeed. They are becoming more important in hiring processes.

The danger in not controlling out-of-class time

· ·

How would you feel if no one was around telling you what you should do when you're not in class? *"Wow!"* You say, *"That would be great!"* **That's the freedom of college:** to decide how to use your out-of-class time. And it's particularly dangerous for students who are drawn to certain distracting activities.

These students abuse their freedom and damage their grades so badly that they have to quit school — or they are asked to leave.

It's a problem of addiction. What kind of addictions am I talking about? Social media, watching movies on devices, playing digital games, texting, talking on the phone, playing cards online, staying up half the night talking to friends — or worse, partying several nights a week. Students get carried away doing what they enjoy doing — because no adult is looking over their shoulder telling them, "That's enough."

If you think "addiction" is too strong a word, you're wrong. We know that drinking and drugs can be addictive, but students who spend 25 hours a week on their devices have a serious problem, too.

I once met a student, a video gamer, who played games **19 hours a day**. He didn't go to class. He didn't sleep much. He also denied that he had a problem. *People with addictions always do.*

I've met these students. They devote all their time and energy to satisfying their addictions. They are out of control. **Start now to learn how to balance your freedom with your responsibility.** It's your future. Don't mess it up because you can't control yourself.

A BONUS FOR PARENTS!
A GUIDE TO SHOPPING FOR
COLLEGES & UNIVERSITIES

H ere's what you and your child should know about the shopping process.

Summer is a good time to visit. It's a convenient time for the entire family. And because colleges offer courses during the summer months, you can visit classes and talk to students.

HOW SOON TO START VISITING CAMPUSES?

You could start as early as the summer after your student's sophomore year—although most students visit colleges during the summer after their junior year. Naturally, you can visit colleges any time of the year — as long as students are present on campus. Don't visit between semesters and during holidays. You want to talk to students while you're there.

WHY VISIT?

True, every college has a website that presents all its exciting features to inform and impress you. So why visit colleges in person? Would you buy a house without walking through it from attic to basement looking at all the rooms and in all the corners and closets? Of course not.

The same is true of "buying" a college — especially considering the financial investment you will make in your child's college education. When you select a college, you want to choose one that you've examined from top to bottom. Just because you like a college's football team, doesn't mean you'll like the college academically. Just because a friend or relative really likes a particular college does not mean your student will.

You want to check out colleges in person, not just look at photographs of buildings and happy students online. Visiting colleges is a very important part of selecting a college. It helps you discover the college that fits your child and his or her personality. So take your college visits seriously and plan for them carefully.

WHAT YOU CAN/SHOULD LEARN FROM WEBSITES.

College sites are filled with good basic information that you should study before you visit. As you look at websites, take notes about questions you want to ask. It's a kind of homework you should do to get prepared before visiting any college. You want to use your time well while you're there — and get all your questions answered. As you study the website, here is what to look for.

What majors (areas of study) and degree programs does the college or university offer? Are they ones your student's interested in? If not, together, you and your child should cross the school off your list.

- what are the admission requirements? Does your child meet them?
- high school courses needed?
- high school grade point average needed?
- SAT and ACT scores required?

- any special admission requirements like application essays, interviews, and number of recommendations?

Of course, you want to know about cost: tuition, room, and board — and what scholarships and financial aid are available to pay for these items. College is expensive. There's no question about that. But remember: Research shows that during a lifetime of earning, a person with a college degree makes twice the amount of money as a person without one. And a college degree makes job and career flexibility easier.

HOW MANY COLLEGES SHOULD YOU VISIT?

Even before you make any college visits, talk as a family about the colleges that interest you and your student: why they might be right. You might bring this conversation to a high school counselor to get his or her opinion.

DON'T SETTLE ON JUST ONE COLLEGE.

BIG MISTAKE. Even if you have a first choice in mind, you can make a good final decision only by comparing it with at least two others. Many students look at and apply to as many as five or six colleges. Your student may not believe this, but it's true: *You can be happy at several colleges if you chose them carefully.* Plus, the Internet makes applying to multiple colleges simpler.

CHOOSE CAREFULLY.

Did you know that 1 out of 4 college freshmen do not return sophomore year to the college in which they first enrolled? It's a huge number. Some students don't return after the first semester.

One reason is that students don't like the college that they chose. Why? They didn't know enough about the school before they chose it. Now these students have to reapply to another college and hope that all of their credits transfer. If the credits don't transfer, the student has just extended the length and cost of their education.

WORKING WITH THE ADMISSIONS OFFICE

- Arrange your visit through the school's admissions office.
- Call or email this office, and get the name of an admissions counselor. This is your contact person going forward.
- Ask if you will receive printed information before your visit.
- Let the counselor know that you want to visit several different offices. (See below.) Ask the counselor to set up appointments for you with these offices.
- While many college admissions offices try to answer all the questions students and parents have, insist on speaking to people in particular offices because their special knowledge of certain areas will make you better informed. Plus, it's always helpful to have the names of particular college officials to contact them when questions occur to you after your visit.
- About a week before the visit approaches, confirm your visit with this counselor by e-mail.

Two essential questions <u>your student</u> should ask of the admissions counselor.

Let your *student* talk to the people you visit on campus. This is a transition time. Students must begin to share responsibility for their education. Plus, your student should prepare questions to ask people you talk to on campus.

Here are the first two questions **your student should ask** of an admissions counselor.

1. *"Given my grade point average, SAT and/or ACT scores and the high school courses I've taken, am I acceptable for admission?"* The Internet will have given you general information. Here is where you discover your student's real chances for admission.

2. *"Given my academic qualifications, what will we have to pay each year, factoring in possible scholarships, the family's annual income, financial aid, and personal expenses?"* Students should know what the family will be spending on their college degree. The amount

being invested in this education should add to your child's serious-
ness of purpose as a student.

Your admissions counselor will answer general questions about everything from the application process to financial aid.

If you have a certain degree program and major in mind, the counselor should
arrange a meeting with a person who represents that area. If you have more than
one area of study in mind, visit as many offices and people as you need to.

Know this: Although some high-ranking colleges require an interview
as part of the application process, a college visit does not constitute an
interview. Nevertheless, when you visit any college, think of it as an interview because the admission counselor you meet may record computer
notes about your visit. These will eventually become part of your student's
application file. So think of each college visit like an interview for a job
you really want. If your child can enter into the discussion, ask good questions, speak well, and make a good impression, these will likely be noted in
the file. The potential student should not sit silently by.

MAIN PLACES TO VISIT ON CAMPUS

Besides the Admissions Office, these are the other particular offices
you should visit:

- Financial Aid
- Academic Advising
- College Degree/Major Office
- Residence Life
- Career Counseling
- Academic Affairs
- Campus Security

Financial Aid

Even though your admissions counselor can offer some information
about covering college costs, you need to talk to a financial aid counselor/

official to get an estimate about college cost, specifically in light of your family's income.

Academic Advising

Academic advisers are assigned to all new students, usually through a central office or through an individual college in a university, like Journalism, for example.

These advisers guide students concerning the selection of courses, choosing a major, or changing a major, and getting through any rough spots. Some colleges use volunteer faculty as advisers. *The best advising is offered through a central office with full time professional academic advisers. The best colleges have excellent advising services. Students need them.*

Degree/Major Offices

When you apply for admission, you will have to indicate what major(s) you're interested in and that will determine the specific college within a university in which your student will enroll. Have good questions in mind when you visit these offices. In particular, you will want to know what job opportunities your student will have after graduating.

If you've selected a major in the sciences or engineering or areas that include laboratory and technical instruction, make sure you see those facilities. You want to know that they are up to date and well equipped.

Residence Life

Because your child will likely live at college, the comforts and convenience of living take on a new meaning. A Residence Life official should be able to answer your questions about how comfortable a sincere learner will be in a particular dorm. Do residence halls have student study lounges? Or do serious students have to find other quiet locations to study outside of dorms? Where do students typically study?

Some other questions: What does your child do if he/she has roommate problems? Do residence halls serve healthy food? What are the dorm rules? Also, after sophomore year, a student may want to live off campus. What service does Residence Life provide for students renting apartments?

Campus safety

Visit the college security office and get information about campus crime and student vulnerability. Safety issues are a reality of college life that must be taken seriously. Colleges are required to provide crime statistics to anyone who wants them. Make sure you do.

Student Affairs

This office manages the non-academic areas of student life — everything from sports activities to social and volunteer activities; from spiritual development to healthy living. Find out what organizations and activities are offered.

Career Counseling

Colleges that are interested in their students' success after graduation have a well-staffed Career Services Office dedicated to career guidance and job application. These offices invite companies looking to hire graduates with various majors to visit campus and interview.

Important: Make sure the Career Office handles liberal arts graduates if your student is going to be in this college. You're expecting this education to take your student somewhere, so you're looking for support for liberal arts grads, too. These grads are good thinkers, problem solvers, analysts, communicators, and innovators. They are able to work in many fields.

Areas of Intended Study

Ask your counselor to arrange a class visit in major areas of study that interest your child. Otherwise, visit a class typically taken by freshmen — like English, History, or Foreign Language.

Ask lots of questions

Do your homework. Study college websites. Ask as many questions as you can while you're there. Parents will have questions, but make sure that, as a prospective student, your child does plenty of talking. Here are some questions your student should ask. Be sure your student brings this list. It gives your student talking points during important meetings and visits.

- How many students graduate on time (four years for a four-year program)? Remember: You want a graduation rate for the particular area you will be enrolled in, not just for the whole college or university.
- What is the rate of job placements for graduates?
- What are your chances of getting scholarships or grants?
- How much financial aid will you qualify for, given your family's income?
- How many students drop out after one year?
- When registering for courses, what happens when a course closes due to full enrollment, and it's a course you need to stay on a degree track? This is an important question. The answer may translate into added expenses for you.
- What extra personal costs will you encounter?

WHAT'S ENTAILED IN YOUR VISIT — TWO VISITS IN ONE.

To prepare for your college visits, your student should create an academic profile for him/herself and take it along to show the various people you meet.

The profile should include a copy of your child's high school transcript and records of standardized test scores, like the PSAT, PLAN, ACT, and/or SAT. The profile should also show courses your student plans to take to finish his or her high school program.

A college education is a family matter. You must be part of the visits and the final selection decision. Make sure you, as a parent, accompany your child when you visit a college. You'll have your own questions to ask.

- Be with your student when talking about college costs.

- Plan your visit for two days, or at least a day and a half.
- Your visit should consist of two different experiences.

1. *The experience conducted by the Admissions Office*

The staff will want to show you the college and campus, sort of like looking at a new, shiny car in a show room. This campus tour is guided usually by a student and arranged by the Admissions Office. Again, remember that this is just a general tour to see campus highlights, like the library, a residence hall, the recreation center, a new classroom building, and so forth. At this point, you should be given a campus map. If not, ask for one.

While on the tour, mark various places on your campus map that you want to visit later on your own. Maybe jot down questions you'd like to ask about them during the tour.

While your tour guide is like a "car salesperson" for the college, be sure you still ask your guide why he or she chose this college. Is it living up to expectations?

2. *The experience you conduct on your own*

The second part is looking at all those areas that really define the quality of a college. That means you need to test drive that car!

While I've listed the other offices you should visit earlier in this guide, you'll want to strike out to investigate on your own. Because you want to visit several offices on campus during this part, make sure you have a map of the college and become familiar with it. Stop in. Ask questions that are both general and pertain to your family. Be sure to talk to areas that relate to a possible major or area of study.

DETERMINING THE QUALITY OF A COLLEGE/UNIVERSITY

Consider these 3 points

1. How well did the college treat you? Assess its service and attitude
    — from the helpfulness of the Admissions Office, to the quality

of Academic Advising for new students, to helping students find a major or a degree program.

2. How much will the college help your student stay on track to complete a degree in four years? This question goes to the quality of advising and their course scheduling — offering needed courses *when your student needs them,* so as not to slow down your child's progress by a semester or two.

3. How much will the college help your student decide on a career and find a job in that area when he or she graduates?

Always keep in mind the amount of money your family will pay for this college education. Make sure you get what you pay for, from start to finish.

PUTTING IT ALL IN PERSPECTIVE

College is not just the next step in an education. It's a giant leap. Professors will expect your student to be a focused, determined, and mature student. The particular college you finally choose should, therefore, be one that will bring out the best of your student's intellectual and personal qualities for the future that awaits.

You need to visit colleges and examine them carefully for yourself. They are all different, and those differences will affect achievement. So make sure you know what you're looking for in a college, visit some schools, and ask intelligent questions to find out if they're right for you.

Beware: This choice cannot be made based just on someone else's recommendation or from a distance like a website. Just because the neighbors' teen "liked it there" or your Uncle Jack graduated from there, isn't a recommendation. All people are different in their preferences and their personalities. What's great for one is not necessarily good for another. Get on campus and get a feel for it.

Made in the USA
Las Vegas, NV
02 September 2021